WRITING
FOR THE
PRESS

WRITING
FOR THE
PRESS

AN INTRODUCTION

James Aitchison

HUTCHINSON
London Sydney Auckland Johannesburg

Hutchinson Education
An imprint of Century Hutchinson Ltd,
62-65 Chandos Place, London WC2N 4NW

Century Hutchinson Australia (Pty) Ltd
89-91 Albion Street, Surry Hills,
New South Wales 2010, Australia

Century Hutchinson New Zealand Ltd
PO Box 40-086, Glenfield, Auckland 10,
New Zealand

Century Hutchinson South Africa (Pty) Ltd
PO Box 337, Bergvlei 2012, South Africa

First published 1988
Reprinted 1989

Set in 10pt Trump Mediaeval

Typeset by Hope Services, Abingdon, Oxon
Printed and bound in Great Britain by
Courier International Ltd, Tiptree, Essex

British Library Cataloguing in Publication Data

Aitchison, James
Writing for the press.
1. Journalism–Manuals
I. Title
070

ISBN 0-09-182252-1

CONTENTS

PREFACE

Writing For The Press began as a series of teaching notes and handouts written to meet the training needs of students on the Higher National Diploma course in Journalism Studies at Napier Polytechnic of Edinburgh.

The Napier Polytechnic course was introduced in 1984, and some of the textbooks available at that time — by F. W. Hodgson, Leslie Sellers and the outstanding series by Harold Evans — offered valuable insights into journalism, but there was no book which could serve as a practical guide for journalism students and trainees, no step-by-step introduction to the essential skills, techniques and forms of journalism.

This lack of an introductory textbook in journalism was also noted by Mr Keith Hall, Director of the National Council for the Training of Journalists, who appealed to the colleges and in-company training centres to produce a suitable book. It was in response to this appeal that I rewrote much of my teaching material — explanatory notes, models and simulations, exercises and sample answers — in book form.

I am indebted to my colleague, Mr Gordon Lang, senior lecturer in the Department of Print Media, Publishing and Communication at Napier Polytechnic, for the generous advice and support he gave while the manuscript of *Writing For The Press* was being written.

James Aitchison
1988

ACKNOWLEDGEMENTS

I am grateful to Mr Alan Harding of the Department of Communication and Media Studies at Highbury College of Technology, Portsmouth for his many helpful comments on the manuscript of *Writing For The Press*, and to students of Journalism Studies at Napier Polytechnic of Edinburgh for testing much of the material in this book.

FOREWORD

Most journalists — and, indeed, many broadcasters — start their careers as trainee reporters with provincial newspapers or news agencies. They receive their basic training through the industry's official scheme, run by the National Council for the Training of Journalists.

Reading is an essential discipline and, we hope, a pleasure to the 2,000 trainees who are registered with the National Council at any one time. So it is — or should be — to thousands of aspiring journalists as they prepare to compete for such trainee vacancies and pre–entry course places as arise each year.

Dr James Aitchison's book, *Writing For The Press*, is a valuable addition to the range of reading available. It is welcomed as such by the National Council, of which he is an advisory member.

Writing For The Press covers many of the requirements of the Council's Newspaper Journalism syllabus.

There are several distinctive features to this book. Each main topic is accompanied by illustrative examples or case studies, and most chapters end with a series of practical training exercises. Although the author is mainly concerned with news values, he never loses sight of the wider human values in society; he is aware of the needs of the newspaper reader as well as the training needs of the young reporter.

Writing For The Press will be an asset to countless trainees for years to come.

Keith Hall
Director
National Council for the Training of Journalists

NOTE ON THE NATIONAL COUNCIL FOR THE TRAINING OF JOURNALISTS

The National Council for the Training of Journalists was founded, under another name, as a result of the 1949 Report of the Royal Commission on the Press. The Report said this about recruitment and training:

> The problem of recruiting the right people into journalism, whether from school or university, and of ensuring that they achieve and maintain the necessary level of education and technical efficiency, is one of the most important facing the Press, because on the quality of the individual journalist depends not only the status of the whole profession, but the possibility of bridging the gap between what Society needs from the Press and what the Press is at present giving it.

The training scheme was established and it has flourished for more than 35 years. Every trainee is required to attend a formal vocational training course or courses; pass a sequence of preliminary examinations, complete a specified period of in-office training and on-the-job practical experience, and pass the NCTJ's National Proficiency Test to become a fully qualified journalist.

NEWS AND NEWS VALUES

News is a record of change in the life of a society, a record of events and incidents, achievements and defeats, arrivals and departures. It is an account of a wide range of developments, some of which may touch directly on the lives of a newspaper's readers while others touch the readers' imagination.

News

Many experienced journalists are understandably reluctant to define news. The accomplished craftsman is sometimes too intimately involved in his craft to be able to step back, look at the subject dispassionately, and then analyse it. A professional journalist's expertise is by definition the result of personal experience, and it is difficult, perhaps impossible, to detach oneself from one's personal experience and discuss that experience objectively. And news writing involves an element of intuition — perhaps the same kind of insight and apprehension that allows the artist or craftsman to see into the possibilities of a subject and to shape that subject to its ideal form — a faculty that resists logical explanation.

It is understandable then that editors and news editors, the people most entitled to discuss the subject, should be unwilling to do so. (A notable exception is Alastair Hetherington, former editor of *The Guardian*, in his book, *News, Newspapers and Television*, published in 1986.) Instead, news editors sometimes speak of having a nose for news, or a flair for it, or a sixth sense. News is difficult to explain, but in a book like this the attempt has to be made.

Most members of society have a natural interest, a healthy curiosity in those changes which affect their personal lives. At a national level many people will be directly affected by a new

1

rate of income tax or the outcome of a general election, while at the local level many will be affected by a spell of severe weather, a fault in the regional television transmitter, or a strike by workers in the local council cleansing department.

When our lives are touched by events then it is entirely normal that we should wish to know more about these events. Only the most apathetic individuals and the most complacent or moribund societies would choose to remain ignorant of events which were in effect part of their own lives. But our interest extends far beyond the limits of our personal lives. Our imaginations may be caught by news of a cricket match in London, a visit by a member of the Royal Family to a hospital in Edinburgh, or the death of a climber on Snowdon.

Newspapers record these changes and, in providing a continuous public account of change, newspapers make the agents of change accountable or at least identifiable to the public. In this sense a good newspaper, although privately owned, should be operating as a public service. When a newspaper keeps an accurate record of events then politicians, industrialists, sportsmen and criminals will receive their due recognition. Maintaining that record is a highly responsible and demanding task.

News values and human values

One of the first demands to be met is to see that news values are not always the same as normal human values.

The normal human response to a particularly violent crime is a sense of outrage or horror at the crime itself and a feeling of compassion for the victim, but a journalist should not include his own emotional response when he reports the crime. He can quote the opinions of police or medical witnesses at the trial of the accused, and the moral censure of the judge as he passed sentence, but in a factual and impartial news story there is no place for an account of the journalist's personal feelings.

The actual experience of one young reporter on a local newspaper is typical of the kind of dilemma — the choice between news values and other human values — which journalists may have to face throughout their careers. The reporter, a woman aged 20, was covering a sitting of a district

2

court and found that one of the cases — a charge of driving while having consumed more than the legal limit of alcohol — referred to a teacher from a local secondary school. The reporter had been the teacher's pupil and she regarded him with admiration and respect. The teacher, who appeared in person with his solicitor, pleaded guilty. During his brief court appearance the teacher caught the reporter's eye and he gave a slight nod of recognition.

When she got back to the office the young reporter was confused and embarrassed. She told her editor that if she reported the case she would feel she was passing sentence on someone she admired. The editor insisted that she write the story, and he published it in the next edition of the newspaper.

The reporter's confusion and embarrassment was a normal human response which arose from her sense of the conflict between news values and other human values. Her concern for her former teacher was understandable but her inclination to suppress the story was wrong. She attended the court not in her own right as a private individual but as a professional reporter with an immediate responsibility to her editor and a wider and deeper responsibility to the reading public. The information she gained in court was not her personal intellectual property but information gained on behalf of her editor and readers. The editor made the only correct editorial decision.

If facts are suppressed on the grounds that their publication could cause embarrassment to the subject of the story, or to the reporter, then this suppression will lead to a whimsical and erratic form of censorship. The result of such censorship will almost certainly be to deny readers the knowledge of actions and decisions that could have an impact on the lives of the readers or could be of legitimate interest to them. At the same time this whimsical censorship would wrongly protect from public accountability those persons responsible for the actions and decisions.

Newsworthy events must be published even if the stories cause embarrassment to the persons involved in them. And newsworthy events must be published even when publication may cause distress to innocent readers.

A report about bogus workmen operating in a town — thieves or confidence tricksters pretending to be from British

Gas or from the local council — may cause some anxiety to elderly readers, but the distress is more than offset by the protection the newspaper gives through its early warning of the bogus workers. Publication of the story would not only be justified in terms of its news value — which is the only necessary justification for publishing — but also in terms of the public service it provided to readers. But distressing news should still be reported even when it gives no practical benefit to the readers.

The bankruptcy of a local businessman and the subsequent redundancy of his employees, the death of a local clergyman after a long and painful illness, the serious injuries suffered by a young family in a road accident, the conviction of the school teacher for driving with more than the legal limit of alcohol — such stories offer no material or spiritual benefits to the readers, but the stories must be told.

To suppress these stories, even on the well intentioned grounds that they might cause distress to the readers, is to suppress the facts. And facts, as this section has already argued, should be regarded as public rather than the personal intellectual property of a reporter or an editor. To suppress such facts over any length of time would be to misrepresent the truth and give a distorted image of society to the readers. Most readers would see through the distortion and, if they continued to read the newspaper, would regard it as a form of fiction. Those readers who could not see the distortion but thought they were being offered a representative news coverage and a true order of reality would be too innocent, too naïve for their own safety in this world. A newspaper would be doing all its readers a disservice if it suppressed bad news.

Press and people — shared values

Although some news values differ from human values there are vitally important areas where the two are identical. The most obvious example is human life.

Murder, manslaughter (culpable homicide in Scotland), attempted murder, abduction, serious assault — these crimes are widely reported because the press reflects society's belief in

4

the paramount value of human life. And particular attention is given to cases involving children because here again the press reflects society's concern for the safety of the most vulnerable members of society.

But it is not only on issues of life and death that newspapers and society share the same values. As this section has already argued, almost any event which touches people's lives, from the outcome of a general election to a strike by workers in the council cleansing department, will be prominently reported in the press.

A news editor, like an ordinary citizen, will take account of other factors such as the scale of an event and its unexpectedness. The sheer size of an event is not an automatic measure of its importance, but the imagination is more likely to be caught by a motorway pile-up of 20 vehicles than a collision between two vehicles. The news value of an event is often a question of scale, and there are occasions as varied as the huge price of a painting at auction or the enormity of a gas explosion when the entire news value of an event lies in its magnitude.

The gas explosion might have an additional news value in its suddenness. The unexpected, the surprising, or the merely odd event catches our attention by its unpredictability, like snow in June or the unforced resignation of a cabinet minister or an outsider winning against massive odds.

Relative news values

The news story begins not at the beginning of a chain of events but at the end because the main property of news is of course its immediacy. And since news is by definition the latest information on the most recent events, then yesterday's motorway crash, or football match, or trade union dispute has some news value while the most momentous events of history have no news value whatsoever. The news story opens with an account of the final outcome of a completed action or the latest position in a continuing action and only then might the news story attempt to record how the action originated and how it developed.

Imagine, for example, that the Glasgow branch factory of a

national company has made substantial losses in the last two years; as a result of this the company decides to close the Glasgow branch and, in reaction to the company's decision, the workers at the Glasgow branch stage a sit-in at the factory. A news story of this sequence of events would open with an account of the most recent development, the workers' sit-in, even if it were obvious to the reporter and his news editor that the sit-in would be futile.

News has a strictly limited life-span, and the news value of an event diminishes as time passes. If too much time passes before an action is reported — and the interval may be a matter only of a day for a weekly newspaper, or an hour for a daily newspaper — then the action may be seen as social history rather than news.

News is relative in terms of place as well as time. For example, a major change in the municipal housing policy of Stirling District Council would probably be front page news in the *Stirling Observer* and might merit a paragraph at the foot of page 5 of *The Scotsman*, but it is doubtful if the change would be reported in any other newspaper in Britain because the news would have no relevance to the lives of people outside Stirling district. Similarly, a successful fund-raising campaign for a hospital in Cardiff would be news in the *South Wales Echo* and the *Western Mail* but not in any other British newspaper.

The limits of a local or regional newspaper's circulation area are normally the limits of its news coverage and the limits of its readers' interest. Proximity of place, like immediacy of time, is an important element in the news value of an event.

In national daily or Sunday newspapers there is the same geographical relativity on a larger scale. British readers are more likely to be interested in British than in foreign news. And the question of foreign news coverage raises other relative values in the national press.

The broadsheet 'quality' press gives more space to foreign news than does the tabloid 'popular' press. Similarly, the broadsheets have a more extensive coverage of politics, financial affairs and education than the tabloids; conversely, the tabloid press gives proportionally more space to entertainment and show business, especially television, to crime and to sport than the broadsheet press. These differences reflect social

6

and intellectual differences in the readership of national newspapers, and editorial judgements are frequently made, not in terms of the absolute news values of stories, but in terms of the stories' relevance to the social class and intellect of the newspapers' readers.

Local newspapers are less concerned than nationals with social and intellectual differences. The local newspaper is written for all sections of the society in which it circulates, and to that extent the good local newspaper — one that records local developments in an accurate, impartial and representative way — can help to promote a sense of community in its circulation area and can thus be a socially cohesive force.

News values are relative not only in terms of the geography, social class and intellect of a newspaper's readers. The values change as society itself changes; that is, the values have a historical relativity.

During the last 20 to 25 years most British newspapers have increased their coverage of economic and financial affairs, of local government and the tensions between local and central government, and of higher education. In the same period there has been an increased coverage, and a more mature coverage, of women's interests, and a greater frankness about sexual matters.

In all these subject areas newspapers have altered their news values in order to reflect changes in British society. Newspapers have followed rather than initiated these developments, although once the developments begin to be reported in the press and other news media then the changes may spread more widely and the rate of change may accelerate.

Ingrown news values

News values may not always be the same as other human values, but if a reporter and news editor allow too wide a gap to grow between the two, or if they become preoccupied by news values to the exclusion of all other values, then there is a risk that the news values will become ingrown.

The risk is greater for large daily newspapers than it is for local newspapers. The local paper has a smaller and more precisely defined readership, the editorial staff usually live within the paper's circulation area, and the editor is often an active member of the community, all of which should mean that the local newspaper is more attentive to the values of the society in which it exists. If a newspaper ignores those values and concentrates exclusively on what it sees as news values, then distortions begin to creep in.

A common distortion is to highlight conflict and controversy while disregarding areas of agreement, and when the element of conflict is exaggerated it follows almost inevitably that personalities will be emphasised at the expense of the underlying issues and policies. Similarly, a newspaper may give greater prominence to stories that contain physical action than to more important stories that contain ideas.

Newspapers rightly keep a close watch on their competitors but they sometimes watch each other so intently that they end up writing the same or similar stories, as when several tabloid newspapers published front page leads on the petty crime of a minor pop singer. News values will always have a tendency to become ingrown if editors do their news-gathering from each other's pages.

But a newspaper can also become trapped by its own particular obsessions. What may have begun as a genuine and highly commendable campaign against illicit drugs or football hooliganism or child abuse may become a wilful determination to find examples of these things where none exist.

Yet another distortion, much more obvious in the national daily and Sunday press than in local weeklies, is the stereotyping — and thus the misrepresentation — of individuals and groups. Stereotyping can all too easily turn ugly. Political, religious or ethnic minorities, social deviants or dissidents who are entirely innocent of any offence may be exposed to public ridicule or even hatred.

These distortions which arise from ingrown news values are comparatively rare in the local press because the local newspaper constantly matches its news values against the wider values of the society it exists to serve. If it ignores those wider values the newspaper may in turn be ignored by those who hold the values, the readers.

Accidental news values

News values can be affected by the physical constraints of newspaper production and the arbitrary nature of life itself.

For reasons of finance, printing technology or trade union agreements, some newspapers may have a maximum number of pages. During an eventful week a local newspaper may gather more news than it can accommodate, in which case some newsworthy material will have to be omitted. In contrast to this there will be quieter weeks when, because of the lack of stronger material, minor stories will have to be given greater prominence than they deserve. And there is always the possibility of an important story breaking just as the newspaper finishes its print run.

NEWS SOURCES AND
NEWS-GATHERING

The reporter on a local newspaper must be aware of
the main sources of news in his newspaper's
circulation area. The reporter should identify reliable
people who have access to these news sources and,
where possible, establish a working relationship
with these people.

News Sources and News-Gathering

The main news sources of a local newspaper are of course the
people and events that make up the life and identity of the
community in which the newspaper circulates. Some news
comes from outside sources — central government and
sometimes local government if the council headquarters are in
another town or city — which affect the life of the local
community, but most news items will come from within the
newspaper's circulation area.

The news values of the reporter on the local newspaper will
sometimes be identical to the news values of the reporter on
the national daily or Sunday. Events such as an important
medical discovery at the local university, the opening of a
major new business, or the closure or takeover of a major
business with possible redundancies, a Royal visit, the resignation or death of the local Member of Parliament and the
consequent by-election, the dismissal of a football club
manager or the transfer of a leading player — events like these
have an absolute news value which would be recognised by any
reporter and almost any reader. But much of the information
that appears in a local newspaper has a relative news value, as
the previous chapter has shown. The information is newsworthy
only in a limited geographical area and may be of little or no

interest outside that area. For example, a local factory's open day or the fixtures and results of the local bowling club league will be of little or no interest to people outside the locality. But these events are of interest to the community in which they occur, and the local newspaper must cover such events if it is to offer wide recognition and a true record of the continuing life of the community.

Some information may not even be news in the strict sense but will be published as a public service: the name and address of the dispensing chemist on duty on Sunday, new opening hours at the local library or forthcoming entertainments in the local cinema and clubs. This willingness to offer a public service, along with the willingness to recognise the life of the entire community, creates a bond between the local newspaper and its readers which a national newspaper cannot achieve.

Among the main sources of news for any local newspaper are local government councils and the courts.

Council

Council meetings must be covered because local government decisions — on housing, education, social services, police and fire services, planning, arts and recreation, environmental health — affect the pattern and quality of our lives. Government of the local community must be open to scrutiny by the community, and the community's only realistic means of scrutinising the council is through regular, accurate newspaper reports of council affairs.

In England and Wales the local newspaper will cover meetings of the parish or community councils, the district council and the county council. In Scotland the local newspaper will cover community councils, district, regional and island councils.

The reporter will attend many of these meetings in person and news-gathering will of course be by shorthand. If news gathered from council meetings has to be supplemented or explained, then the reporter will make a direct personal approach, or more probably a telephone approach, to contacts

11

amongst the elected councillors and the council's full time officials. The reporter should have telephone numbers for the chairmen, chairwomen or conveners of the important committees of the council: housing, education, social services, emergency services, and planning.

Council officials are normally forbidden to talk to the press without the approval of the elected councillors, but the reporter should be able to establish confidential contacts amongst the officials. Although the information gained from these confidential sources is often unattributable or even completely off the record, the information is still worth having if the alternative is ignorance. Council officials and elected councillors might claim that this practice raises questions of loyalty. The answer is that officials, councillors and the local newspaper all share the same ultimate loyalty — to the people, voters and readers, who make up the community.

Members of Parliament

Your Member of Parliament can also be an important source of political news, or more probably a source of comment on the news. The local MP should be asked to explain the local significance of Parliamentary business or the impact a new bill will have on your newspaper's readers. The MP should also be asked to comment on important local issues as they arise, although some MPs who observe the niceties of the central-local government electoral processes may be unwilling to comment on local council affairs.

Court

Court reports have always attracted the interest of British newspaper readers. The interest is understandable; an account of a crime can excite the readers, or horrify or disgust them, and the passing of sentence on a guilty party brings a sense of satisfaction. But behind the drama of crime and punishment lies the deeper concern for law, order and justice in society. Court reports in the local newspaper express, and to some extent satisfy, this deep concern. At the same time court reports meet a fundamental need of a democratic society; the process of law, like that of government, must be open to public scrutiny. Secret law, like secret government, can lead to irresponsibility, corruption and tyranny. The accurate and impartial reporting of court and council, week after week and year after year, is probably the most important service a local newspaper can offer its readers.

Court reporting demands absolute accuracy and impartiality. In some cases the reporter may be entitled to publish nothing at all, and the act of publication could bring a charge of contempt of court. Contempt proceedings could also be brought as a result of a report, especially a biased or inaccurate report, which appeared to pre-judge the court's decision or could affect the outcome of a case. Someone who is wrongly identified as an accused person — or worse, someone who is wrongly identified as a guilty person — may bring an action for libel against the newspaper.

In England and Wales the reporter will cover the Magistrates Court, County Court, the Crown Court and inquests; Juvenile Court should be covered with great caution since it could be contempt of court to reveal the identities of juvenile offenders. In Scotland the reporter will cover the District Court, Sheriff Court and occasionally the High Court; he should also cover fatal accident enquiries, investigations similar to inquests and normally conducted by Scottish sheriffs. Industrial tribunals should also be covered when there is a strong local interest.

Other news sources

Other important sources of news for the local newspaper are the police force, the fire brigade, the ambulance service, the hospital, local industries and businesses and their representative bodies, the chamber of trade or commerce or a traders' association, trades unions and trades councils, and the local football club. Secondary sources are schools and colleges, churches, local clubs and societies and local branches of national pressure groups and charities.

The reporter should make contact with persons in each of these areas. Personal contact is essential in the first instance so that the reporter can clearly identify himself and establish a working, trusting relationship. Once the relationship is established the reporter should maintain contact through regular telephone calls and occasional personal visits.

Your contacts in rural areas could include head teachers of village schools, village postmasters, publicans and hotel-keepers, agricultural merchants, livestock auctioneers and countryside rangers or wardens.

Some newspapers' circulation areas include specialist organisations or centres of specialist activity — coastguard stations, mountain rescue centres, airports, fishing or ferry ports, universities or polytechnics, major tourist attractions — which can be important sources not only of news but of interviews, profiles, news-features and even full-length feature articles.

News releases

In the course of a normal week a local newspaper will probably receive dozens of unsolicited items in the form of news releases, press statements and handouts. These can be a useful source of genuine news but the reporter should treat them with some scepticism because in almost every case the news release offers only the information — usually good news — which the issuing organisation wishes to make known.

Some news releases or handouts will be little more than attempts to get free advertising; in other cases the release will be a well written presentation of hard facts which are of interest to your readers. When a newsworthy release comes from an organisation which you know and trust or from a writer who is known to you then it will often be safe to use the information without further investigation. If you have any doubts about the news release or if you feel the information is incomplete you should of course telephone the organisation which issued the release to ask for more detail, especially detail about the people involved, about the cost in financial terms or in terms of impact on the environment, the real purpose or intention behind the news release and about any possible effect on your newspaper's readers. When you telephone the organisation you should also keep in mind the need for a quote from someone in authority.

Many large organisations and almost all pressure groups and campaigning organisations often have full-time press officers, some of them former journalists, who maintain a regular output of news releases. But most local clubs and societies do not have the resources — the time, the money or the people — to maintain professional links with the press. You and your newspaper can persuade these clubs and societies that a great deal can be done on a part-time, amateur basis.

Your newspaper could publish a statement inviting all local clubs to send copies of their annual programmes of events and meetings and also regular reports of specific events. For those clubs whose members have no experience of press relations you could prepare a simple handout explaining the basic requirements of a good news release, or your editor or chief reporter could invite club secretaries to visit the newspaper office — probably in groups of six to ten in order to make the exercise manageable — to discuss the handout and the basic elements of news writing, as shown in Chapter 3. The editor would explain that it was not possible to send reporters to cover all the events staged by local clubs but if the clubs were to send their own reports — factual, newsworthy accounts that met the newspaper's copy date — then these reports would always be considered for publication.

The benefit for the clubs is that they would probably get additional publicity and with it the chance to increase their memberships. The benefit for the newspaper of course is that it would get an increased flow of local news and probably an increase in the good will of the local clubs. The financial cost to the clubs and the newspaper would be negligible.

Newspaper news

Newspapers can discover genuine news stories in their own classified advertisements. The births, marriages and deaths column — the BMDs — is sometimes the first notification a newspaper gets of a golden wedding anniversary or of the death of a prominent citizen. If the BMD notice is spotted in time there is the possibility of a photograph and story of the golden wedding couple, or an obituary of the dead person, for the next issue of the newspaper.

The situations vacant advertisements may show that a local firm is recruiting staff, and behind the recruitment advertisement there could be a story of the firm's expansion to meet new orders or diversification into new products. A recruitment advertisement by the local council may show that a new post or even a new department is being created; a local newspaper should find out exactly why the new posts are being created and exactly what service they will offer.

Classified advertisements for forthcoming entertainments sometimes show that a well-known actor, musician or comedian will be appearing in the newspaper's circulation area. The newspaper then has the opportunity to review the performance and to interview the performer.

Newspapers can make news in other ways. A newspaper in association with a local firm or a local club can sponsor events for charity — a walk, a half-marathon, a vicars versus police football match, an annual fête or flower show. The paper can launch local campaigns — crime-watch, drugs-watch, keep fit or anti-litter. It can run creative competitions for children or adults in photography, painting or even news writing, and it can run 'easy-to-enter' competitions on its own account or in association with advertisers. The prizes for the competitions would be donated by the advertisers so that there would be no cost to the newspaper.

If a newspaper agrees to sponsor an event then an essential part of the agreement should always be that the time-consuming business of organising the event is the responsibility of the co-sponsor, the local firm or club. The newspaper can then concentrate on what it does best.

These activities can lead to genuine news stories or news pictures; they can also stimulate readers' interest and involvement and so strengthen the bond between the newspaper and the community. The activities might even help to increase the newspaper's circulation.

The diary

The editor and the chief reporter control the news-gathering exercise by means of the diary, normally an A4-size desk diary with a full page per day; the page should be sub-divided into hours of the day or at least into morning, afternoon and evening so that entries can be made in a chronological order.

When a newspaper gets notice about forthcoming events the details — the nature of the event, the time of day, the place, the person or persons involved — are entered in the diary for the appropriate date. That page of the diary then forms a programme of visits and telephone calls for the day. Efficient news-gathering, and thus an efficient newspaper, depends on a well-maintained diary, and it is essential that you advise your editor or chief reporter of any significant forthcoming events that you discover.

Contacts book

It is essential too to maintain an up-to-date contacts book or set of contacts cards.

You should keep an alphabetical list of all your contacts by name, position or job description, address and telephone number. For many of your contacts you should have a home telephone number as well as a business number so that the contact can be reached outside normal working hours, and in these cases it is worth having a cross-reference or double entry, one entry under the name of the organisation and the other under the name of the individual contact.

Your contacts list of councillors, Members of Parliament, press officers, club secretaries, and others will change from time to time and so your contacts list should be based on a simple, flexible system such as a ring-back notebook which allows pages to be added or removed, or a set of index cards. Whatever system you use you should remember that a large, up-to-date contacts list is both a valuable source of news and a means to efficient news-gathering.

3

WRITING THE NEWS

The news story is one of the most disciplined forms of prose writing. The immediacy of the introductory paragraph (the intro), the firmly controlled narrative structure, the strict accuracy, relevance and topicality of information, the economy of language, and the neutrality of the narrative and editorial viewpoint — these features make the news story as distinctive a prose genre as the fictional short story or the scientific report.

The news story

The news story is essentially a story, a self-contained factual narrative, but unlike the story-line of fiction which unfolds until it completes a pattern, the news story normally begins by encapsulating the completed pattern or the main feature of that pattern, and then summarises the incidents or circumstances that create the pattern.

The news story is a report, but unlike the scientific or academic report which reaches its conclusion only after a logical progression through its terms of reference, procedure, and findings, the news story normally begins with the conclusion and then states the main findings that lead to the conclusion. The terms of reference and the procedure would be summarised or omitted.

Some of the factors that have shaped the present form the news story takes in local and broadsheet newspapers are: the need for accuracy, pressure of space, and concern for the reader.

Accuracy is essential if the newspaper is to avoid complaints, including complaints to the Press Council or charges of libel by people whose words and actions are inaccurately reported. Apart from any financial costs arising from a complaint against a newspaper, the act of responding to a complaint can be time-consuming. A well founded complaint against a local newspaper could involve the editor in several hours of telephoning, letter-writing and conciliatory lunching.

But an even stronger drive towards accuracy comes from the sheer professionalism of the good journalist, with his pride in personal craftsmanship and in the standards and reputation of his newspaper. A journalist whose work is constantly inaccurate is a poor journalist, and any newspaper which regularly publishes inaccurate reports becomes an object of ridicule as well as a target for litigation.

Pressure of space in newspapers has led to the compactness of form and the economy of language of the modern news story. This discipline of length demands that the journalist exercises sound judgement in selecting the main facts from any set of circumstances, and it demands that those facts be presented concisely.

Concern for the reader requires that the news story must be immediately intelligible in its structure as well as its language; a news story is worthless if its language cannot be understood or if its story-line lacks cohesion and continuity. And this concern for the reader requires that the narrative viewpoint must be as objective as possible; the news story should not be muddied by opinion, comment, bias or prejudice.

These principles of news writing are illustrated in the news stories that follow.

Consider the following information as the basis of a news story of not more than 200 words for a local weekly newspaper, the Wallfield Mercury.

North Dale School was built in 1878 to accommodate all children aged five to 14 in the North Dale area. Since 1946 it has been the local primary school for children aged five to 11. In the early years of this century, when the school roll was over 200, there were six teachers. In the last five years the roll has averaged 15 pupils and there is now only one teacher.

Last month the Walls and Dalesmoor education committee decided to close the school at the end of the current school year. The decision was confirmed by a full meeting of Walls and Dalesmoor County Council last week.

From next September pupils aged five to 11 in the North Dale area will attend South Dale Primary School seven miles away. A minibus will be provided for the outward and return journeys.

Mrs Jean Hamilton, secretary of the North Dale Parents' Committee, told the Wallfield Mercury: 'The decision is a disgrace. The school is the centre of the community here in North Dale, and if the school closes part of the community will die.

'I'm sure the children will suffer. North Dale is a happy school and it is ridiculous to send children as young as five away from home for their primary schooling.

'The education chairman has refused to meet us but we will fight this decision. The Parents' Committee are organising a petition. We shall also be writing to our MP.'

The information should be written in a form like this:

School closure — 1

Patrick Napier   1 February

North Dale parents' committee will campaign against the closure of North Dale primary school.

more

School closure — 2

Walls and Dalesmoor education committee decided last month to close the school at the end of the current school year, and the decision was confirmed at a full meeting of the county council last week.

Mrs Jean Hamilton, secretary of the North Dale parents' committee, said the decision was a disgrace. 'The school is the centre of the community here in North Dale, and if the school closes part of the community will die.'

more

School closure — 3

Primary school pupils in the North Dale area, where the school roll averages 15, will attend South Dale primary school

20

from next September. A minibus will be provided for the 14-mile round trip.

Mrs Hamilton said the children would suffer and that it was ridiculous to send children as young as five away from home for their primary schooling.

'The education chairman has refused to meet us but we shall fight this decision,' Mrs Hamilton said. 'The parents' committee are organising a petition. We shall also be writing to our MP.'

end

Content

There are major differences of content between this news story and the original material on which it is based.

Most of the information in the first paragraph of the original version has been omitted. The limit of 200 words means that some of the original material has to be cut, and the cuts are made to the secondary information, that is, the historical and background material in the first paragraph. What has been retained from the first paragraph of the original — the fact that the school roll has averaged only 15 pupils in the last five years — is essential for the story since the small number of pupils is clearly the reason for the proposed closure of the school.

The material omitted is not essential for the news story, and in its original position in paragraph one the material delays the discovery of the real news. If the word limit had been 225 or 250 the secondary information might still have been omitted; it would certainly have been relegated to a later paragraph in the story. Historical material, background material, incidental material or any information which has no immediacy of time or place and which contains no news points should be omitted or relegated to a late paragraph in the news story.

It must never appear in the intro (the introductory paragraph) of a news story where it would assume an undue importance and also delay the real news.

News points

The news story consists almost entirely of significant facts:

the name of a person, Mrs Jean Hamilton; the political office of two other persons, the chairman of the education committee and the local MP; the names of places and organisations, North Dale school, South Dale school, Walls and Dalesmoor education committee and Walls and Dalesmoor County Council; political decisions and their consequences on the children and the wider community; and reactions, in the quote from Mrs Hamilton, to those political decisions.

All these facts are important and they should be regarded as news points which must be included in the news story.

On some occasions news points will be immediately identifiable: a dramatic event such as a fire or a road accident; an interesting or unusual set of circumstances such as council elections or a spell of extreme weather; an unexpected incident or development such as the sudden resignation of a councillor, or a successful cup run by the local football club.

News points are not always as dramatic as these, but when the news is less immediately obvious you can use a simple mnemonic. Ask yourself:

Who? What? How? Why? When? and Where?

Think of it as a silent chant:

Who-What-How? Why-When-and-Where?

The intro

In the news story above, the order of the original material has been drastically changed. The story opens with information from the final paragraph and links this with information in the second paragraph of the original in order to create an effective intro, or introductory paragraph. The intro then largely determines the structure of the news story that follows.

Effective intros can take a wide variety of forms but the two main forms are the **comprehensive** and the **specific**.

A comprehensive intro summarises or encapsulates the essence of the story and delivers the main outcome in the opening sentence. A specific intro spotlights a particular fact or incident — the most important, the most recent, or the most unusual — and develops the story from that point.

22

Intros should be immediate, positive and active wherever this is possible without distorting the facts.

The intro should be immediate in the double sense of leading with the most up-to-date information and going directly to the heart of the story, or to a key fact or incident, without hesitation. For example, do not write:

> According to a report published today, British men aged 45 to 55 are healthier than ever before.

The opening words delay the news point and thus reduce its impact. The intro should be written:

> British men aged 45 to 55 are healthier than ever before, according to a report published today.

The intro should be positive because news is a record of change and development rather than the absence of change. Do not write:

> No-one was seriously injured when a coach with 35 holiday-makers was in collision with a lorry south of Inverness last night.

The opening words are negative and seem to tell the reader that nothing happened. The intro should be positive:

> Thirty-five holiday-makers escaped serious injury last night when their coach was in collision with a lorry south of Inverness.

And the intro is more positive when it uses the active rather than the passive voice of the verb. Do not write:

> A national poetry prize has been won by a Glasborough school teacher, Miss Emily Gates.

You achieve a more positive effect, and a more immediate local interest for the readers of the Glasborough Gazette, if you write:

> Glasborough school teacher Miss Emily Gates has won a national poetry prize.

News angles

Consider the intro to the news story above:

> North Dale parents' committee will campaign against the closure of North Dale primary school.

The intro brings together two news points, the parents' decision to organise a campaign and the council's decision to close the school. By bringing the two news points together in this way the intro gains a greater impact and also creates a news angle — the conflict between the parents' committee and the council. The news angle is re-affirmed in the final paragraph of the news story.

A news angle is the narrative standpoint taken by the reporter, or the sub-editor, on the strength of the news points and the news values in the situation on which the story is based. The angle is formed by bringing together two or more news points or news values.

In some cases the news story is so straightforward that there is no real angle. The news story of the death from natural causes of a retired businessman would have no noticeable news angle and might be indistinguishable from an obituary on the dead man. But if the businessman died in suspicious circumstances then the news angle would be formed quite simply by bringing together the facts of his death and of the police investigation. The angle would be more acute if forensic scientists were involved in the investigation or if a post mortem examination were held.

Similarly, a story about a local athlete achieving international success need have no precise news angle other than the local element, but if the athlete had succeeded despite a serious boyhood injury from which doctors said he would not fully recover, then the news angle is formed by bringing together the facts of his success and of his earlier injury.

The narrower or more specific the news angle, the more careful the reporter and sub-editor should be. Since a news angle is a narrative standpoint or viewpoint it is therefore the result of an act of interpretation by the writer or editor, an interpretation which must be justified by the facts of the case. Another reason for caution in the use of narrow news angles is

24

that the angle in the intro should be developed in the continuous narrative flow of the complete story. That is, the intro should determine the nature of the story that follows. But if there are not enough news points to sustain the interpretation implicit in the news angle in the intro then the intro will look isolated and perhaps absurd. The angle may even look like a clumsy attempt to tell the reader what to think.

Quotes

In the original account of the decision to close North Dale school, three of the six paragraphs consisted of one continuous quotation from Mrs Jean Hamilton, but in the news story the continuous quote has been deliberately broken, partly to keep within the 200-word limit but also to achieve the creative tension that comes from the interaction of direct and indirect speech.

The use of quotes in the news story is fully explained in Chapter 8.

Copy presentation

The rules of copy presentation — that is, the way the reporter sets out the text of the story before handing it over to the sub-editor — have been partly overtaken by computers. Electronic typesetting by word processor makes it possible to key in the story and then do the complete sub-editing exercise on screen. The sub-editor can correct copy, decide the line-spacing and column width, select the size, style and face of type, plan the layout of each page, and finalise the copy-fitting.

But even in an age of rapidly changing technology the journalist is expected to know the rules of copy presentation. Some newspapers have not yet introduced electronic type-setting while others have introduced it as a two-stage process in which the journalist types the story and then, when the story has been sub-edited, the electronic keyboard operator — sometimes a compositor who has been retrained in the new technology — sets the story for printing.

Most of these rules are illustrated in the news story on the closure of North Dale school, and the rules are explained here.

Byline and date

At the top of the first page, or folio, of the news story is the reporter's name, or byline, Patrick Napier, and the date when the story was written. The term 'byline' — quite simply, who the story was written by — is normally used only when the reporter's name appears in print, but the term is also used at the pre-publication stage when it is essential to know who wrote which stories so that facts can be checked, or additional information included, or a follow-up story written for the next issue of the newspaper. The date, of course, tells the sub-editor when, and for what issue of the newspaper the story was written.

Catchline

At the top right of the first folio is the catchline, 'School closure — 1', at the top right of the second folio the catchline is 'School closure — 2', and at the top right of the third folio is 'School closure — 3'. The catchline is normally a single word, repeated on each folio of the story, which allows the sub-editor or the typesetter to identify a story immediately. Some sub-editors insist that the catchline should be a word which appears in the intro of the story.

The number alongside the word is in effect the page number, or folio number, of the news story in its raw copy state before it appears in the newspaper. Strict numbering is essential, especially in a long story, so that the typesetter can set the copy in the correct sequence.

Since the purpose of the catchline is to identify the story at a glance, the reporter must use an appropriate word. Words like 'Council', 'Court', 'Police', 'Theft', 'Accident', 'Fire', 'Hospital' or 'Prize', are not safe catchlines because there could be two or more stories on these subjects in a single issue of a local newspaper. If one word is not enough to identify your story then you must use two words, as in the news story on North Dale school — 'School closure' — where no single word in the intro can be used as a safe catchline.

Words which are part of newspaper jargon, especially words which indicate a sub-editor's decision on a story, must never be used as catchlines because they could easily be mistaken for instructions. These words include 'Flash', 'Rush', 'Splash', 'Hold', 'Spike', 'Kill', 'Leader', 'Bold' and 'Sub'.

Line spacing

You must always have generous spacing throughout your typescript so that the sub-editor can write instructions to the typesetter. General guidelines on spacing are:

- The top three or four inches of the first folio of your story should be left blank.
- Allow a left-hand margin of two inches and a right-hand margin of one inch.
- Allow maximum spacing between the lines of your copy so that the sub-editor can re-write parts of the story or write particular typesetting instructions between the lines.
- Each folio should begin with a new paragraph and end with a completed paragraph. Never break a paragraph across two pages because this slows down the processes of sub-editing and typesetting.
- Some editors insist that the opening paragraph, the intro, be written on a separate folio. This is indicated in the news story on the school closure above.
- If a story continues over two or more folios, write 'more', or 'more follows', or 'mf' after the final paragraph on the folio. When you begin a new folio you will of course include the correct folio number in the catchline.
- After the final paragraph of the final folio write 'end'.

These guidelines on spacing and copy presentation reinforce the meaning of the story. If the guidelines are not followed then the sub-editing and typesetting stages of the production process become more complicated — and more foul-tempered — than they need be.

The reporter can make the meaning of the story even clearer, and the production process even simpler, if these additional guidelines on copy presentation are followed:

- Errors in typing or spelling should be clearly deleted and the word or words should be rewritten, if necessary above the line.
- Words should never be abbreviated unless the abbreviation

is widely understood. Even the simplest of abbreviations can sometimes be ambiguous. For example, Dr can be Doctor or Drive; St can be Saint or Street; Ms can be a feminine term of address or manuscript.

- Similarly, never refer to an organisation simply by the initial letters of its name unless you have clearly indicated the name and the initials to the reader. Thus:

   The Campaign for Nuclear Disarmament (CND) will hold an evening rally in Wallfield on Wednesday 4 March.

- The words 'today', 'yesterday' and 'tomorrow' should never be used alone; the name of the day should always be added. Thus:

   Fire destroyed three classrooms at Wallfield High School yesterday, Thursday.

   and:

   Glasborough Art Club's annual exhibition opens tomorrow, Saturday, in Victoria Hall.

- The numbers from one to nine should be written in alphabetical characters. Numbers from 10 upwards should be written in numerals. It is much easier to write and to read £11,786,734 than to write or read eleven million, seven hundred and eighty-six thousand, seven hundred and thirty-four pounds.

- Upper case (capital, or caps) letters should be used only for names (proper nouns), and only when the name is given in full. Lower case letters should be used elsewhere. Thus:
   Glasborough District Council met last night.
   but:
   The council elected a new chairman.
   Similarly:
   Walls and Dalesmoor Police have issued a statement.
   but:
   The police statement appeals for witnesses.

- Finally, never try to 'assist' the sub-editor by marking up your own copy for typesetting. Your efforts could cause confusion and resentment.

News story exercises

Consider this example.

Use the following information to write a news story of 100 to 150 words for the Wallfield Mercury, which is published each Thursday.

> The Reverend Malcolm Seaton has been minister of St Ninian's Methodist Church, Wallfield, for 22 years.
>
> His wife died last year after a long illness. He has two children and three grandchildren.
>
> In the last 10 years he has raised over £80,000 for the Methodist Hospice in Wallfield which can now accommodate up to 30 terminally ill patients.
>
> On Friday of last week he was convicted of driving with more than the legal limit of alcohol in his blood. He was fined £250 and banned from driving for a year.
>
> Before he entered the church he was an outstanding athlete. He held the British record for the 100 and 220 yards from 1948 to 1951, and he won seven caps in England's rugby team during the same period.
>
> He has stated that he intends to resign from the church because of his offence.
>
> Mr Seaton was only 100 yards from his home when he was stopped by the police. No other vehicle was involved and no one was injured.

Here is a news story based on the information above.

Patrick Napier   7 April

Methodist — 1

A local Methodist minister says he intends to resign from the church because of his conviction for a drink-driving offence.

more

Methodist — 2

The Reverend Malcolm Seaton, minister of St Ninian's Methodist Church, Wallfield, was convicted last Friday of driving with more than the legal limit of alcohol in his blood. He was fined £250 and banned from driving for one year.

29

Minister at St Ninian's for 22 years, Mr Seaton was only 100 yards from his home when he was stopped by the police. No other vehicle was involved and no one was injured.

In the last 10 years he has raised over £80,000 for Wallfield's Methodist Hospice, which can now accommodate up to 30 terminally ill patients.

Mr Seaton, whose wife died last year, has two children and three grandchildren. Before he entered the church he was an outstanding sportsman, representing England seven times at rugby and holding the British record for the 100 and 220 yards.

end

Use the following information to write a news story of 250 to 300 words for the Glasborough Gazette, which is published each Friday.

On 1 February Mr Philip Border, Secretary of the Glasborough Branch of the Campaign for Nuclear Disarmament (CND), wrote to the Chief Officer of Glasborough District Council and to the Chief Superintendent of the Glasborough Division of Chalklands Police Force informing them that Glasborough CND intended to hold a torchlit procession and rally — a March for Peace — in Glasborough on Wednesday 5 March from 7.30 pm to 9 pm. Mr Border enclosed a street plan showing the route of the procession from the Old Corn exchange, along the High Street to Victoria Square. Both the District Council and the Police agreed to the proposal.

On Saturday 1 March Wallfield United and Glasborough City drew two-all in the third round of the FA Cup. The replay was scheduled for Glasborough's ground, King's Park, at 7.30 pm on Wednesday 5 March.

There was a capacity crowd of 35,000 at King's Park on the Wednesday evening, and hundreds of Wallfield fans were locked out. The angry fans stood chanting outside the ground for some minutes and then headed for the city centre.

The CND march left the Old Corn Exchange shortly after 7.30 pm. Half way along the High Street six police officers tried to divert the marchers into Palmerston Place. Mr Border tried to push past the police and was detained. Police and CND stewards eventually persuaded the other marchers to disperse.

Later that evening Councillor Charles Rodney, who lives in

Victoria Square, told the Gazette: 'Dozens of Wallfield fans who could not get into King's Park went on the rampage. A chanting mob gathered in Victoria Square. Shop windows were broken and there was some looting. Several cars were damaged and one car was overturned. I think some fans tried to set fire to the overturned car but the police moved in quickly to stop them. I don't think any residents were hurt.'

Chief Superintendent Trevor Ashton of the Glasborough Division of Chalklands Police said: 'Because of the disorder in Victoria Square we had to divert the CND march, largely for the safety of the marchers. Five people, three of them police officers, were slightly injured. Eleven people, ten of them from Wallfield, were arrested and detained. One man was detained and later released.

When the Gazette telephoned Mr Philip Border the next day he said: 'I now understand what the police were trying to do, but the situation last night was very confused. After all, our route was approved by the police a month ago. I knew nothing about the disturbance in Victoria Square until I was taken to the police station where I saw some of the fans who had been arrested. I was released after about an hour. It is tragic that our March for Peace was halted by football hooligans.'

Mr Harry Horton, Chairman of Wallfield United Football Club, told the Gazette: 'I'm sorry about the trouble last night, but it wouldn't have happened if Glasborough had made it an all-ticket replay.'

The replay ended in a win for Wallfield by three goals to two.

Use the following information to write a news story of 200 to 250 words for the Glasborough Gazette, which is published each Friday.

The Glasborough Health Authority authorised a £1.85m modernisation programme for Queen Mary's Hospital, Glasborough. The hospital has 85 beds for geriatric patients and also provides day care for 60 to 100 elderly persons, including disabled persons, each week.

The contract for renovation and repair was awarded to Harold Rae & Sons, Building Contractors, Glasborough, on the understanding that the hospital would remain in continuous use during the work; patients would be moved from ward to ward as the work progressed.

On Monday of this week, three weeks after the work started,

the residential patients were dispersed to old folks' homes throughout the Glasborough area, and provision for day care patients at Queen Mary's Hospital ceased.

Yesterday morning a member of the hospital staff telephoned the Gazette in confidence and said that the patients had been evacuated because dangerous blue asbestos had been found in several wards.

The Gazette telephoned Glasborough Health Authority immediately. A spokeswoman denied the story. She said: 'The patients have been withdrawn to allow work to proceed more quickly.' She refused to make any further statement.

When the Gazette telephoned Harold Rae & Sons, Mr James Rae, a partner in the firm, said: 'Yes, it's blue asbestos all right. My men found it in the first week and I reported it to the administration at Queen Mary's and to the District Council Environmental Health Department. An administrative officer at Queen Mary's said it would take them a week or two to arrange alternative accommodation for the old folk. The environmental health men came down. They said they weren't very happy about the situation but told us we could carry on if we took all the precautions. You know, seal off the ward we're working in at the time, coat the asbestos before removing it, and give the men approved safety masks and goggles. So that's what we did.'

The Gazette telephoned the Health Authority spokeswoman again. She said: 'I now understand that blue asbestos has in fact been found in Queen Mary's. Work went on for a week or so after the discovery because there was no other accommodation for the patients, and we didn't want to cause undue alarm. Stringent safety measures were observed and the patients were never at risk.'

Dr Andrew Pressler of the Department of Materials Science at Glasborough University said: 'There is always an element of risk in dealing with this material. I don't know exactly what precautions were taken on this occasion but it is not advisable to remove asbestos if unprotected people are on or near the premises.'

Write a news story of 250 to 300 words for the Scottish weekly newspaper, the Airdshire Advertiser, which is published each Wednesday. (You can assume that some of the information has already appeared in the Advertiser, and that it can be used again in your full version of the story.)

On 21 April Mr Angus Lochrie, owner of a 1,200-acre hill farm near Glen Aird, Airdshire, applied to Newton Aird District Council for planning permission to build 25 holiday chalets on a site adjoining Loch Aird. The chalets would be built on Mr Lochrie's land by John Cameron & Sons, Builders, of Newton Aird.

The Planning Department of the District Council publicised the application and invited comments. The District Council also advised the Regional Council Planning Department of the application.

Glen Aird Community Council submitted a written objection to the application, stating: 'The development would be detrimental to an area of great natural beauty.'

Newton Aird Planning Department, at its meeting on 26 May, refused planning permission. The convener of the planning committee, Councillor Hamish McCrindle, stated: 'Planning permission is refused on the grounds that the development would be detrimental to an area of outstanding scenic beauty; the 25 chalets would constitute an over-development of the site; the development would pose an unacceptable srain on existing services, notably roads, water and drainage; and the proposed development is outside the local structure plan.'

Mr Lochrie exercised his right to appeal to the Secretary of State.

Mr William Watson, an inspector appointed by the Secretary of State, called a site meeting at Loch Aird of all interested parties for 3 September. Those present at the site meeting were: Mr Angus Lochrie, the appellant; Mr Iain Cameron of John Cameron & Sons; Councillor Hamish McCrindle, convener of the District Council Planning Committee; Mr Alfred Houston, assistant director of the District Council Planning Department; Mr Graham Morse, director of the Regional Council Roads Department; Mr Kenneth Hunter, assistant director of the Regional Council Water and Drainage Department; Mrs Morag Baxter, secretary of the Glen Aird Community Council; and a reporter from the Airdshire Advertiser.

During the site meeting Mr McCrindle and Mrs Baxter repeated their previous objections. Mrs Hamilton added: 'All these incomers would upset the existing community in the Glen Aird area.'

Mr Angus Lochrie said: 'What's the point of having an area of outstanding scenic beauty if it's seen only by me, my dogs and the damned sheep? Loch Aird is ideal for holiday homes.'

Mr Iain Cameron said: 'The development will bring tourist

income and employment to the area. My firm will guarantee to build a road linking the chalets to the Glen Aird road. We will also install water and drainage, in co-operation with the Regional Council. It's nonsense to say that 25 chalets on a twelve hundred acre farm constitutes over-development of the site.'

Mr Morse and Mr Hunter both said the regional council had no objection to the proposals.

On Thursday 27 October Newton Aird Planning Department received a letter from the Scottish Development Department (SDD) stating that the Secretary of State, on the advice of his inspector, Mr William Watson, had over-ruled the planning department and given permission for the Loch Aird development to proceed.

The SDD letter stated the Secretary of State's decision was final. Copies of the letter were sent to all persons who had attended the site meeting. Mr Iain Cameron telephoned the Airdshire Advertiser and disclosed the contents of the letter.

Use the following information to write a news story of 200 to 250 words for next week's issue of the Wallfield Mercury, which is published each Thursday.

Last week Mr Philip Landsman and Mr Walter Crane, teachers of physical education at King Edward's School, Wallfield, took a group of pupils hill-walking during the Easter holiday. The group, 20 boys aged 15 to 16, were based at the North Dale adventure hostel, Dalesmoor. At the end of the week there was an incident involving three of the boys.

Mr Walter Crane said: 'The weather was cold but as the days passed the boys completed longer walks and held orienteering competitions. The group spent the last afternoon in the town of South Dale, and that night the boys held an impromptu party and concert.

'Three boys were missing at breakfast the next morning. The other boys said the three had gone out after the concert without saying where they were going.'

Mr Philip Landsman said: 'Mr Crane and ten boys formed a search party; the other boys remained in the hostel with me. When Mr Crane had not returned after two hours, I telephoned the police at South Dale, and the sergeant there called out the Dalesmoor Rescue Team.

'The Rescue Team found the three after an hour or so and took them to South Dale Hospital. All three were suffering slightly from exposure but no one was injured. They will be released tomorrow.'

Mr Crane added: 'As the senior member of staff I accept full responsibility for the incident. I've telephoned the parents of the three boys, and my headmaster, to explain the situation and to let them know we will be a day late in returning to Wallfield. I've also spoken to Sergeant Spiller, who has been very helpful.'

Sergeant Mike Spiller of Walls and Dalesmoor Police, leader of the Dalesmoor Rescue Team, said: 'It was a silly dare that could have ended in tragedy. The three lads challenged each other to a race round the North Dale Crags in the dark, and they set off late last night, leaving their equipment and waterproof clothing in the hostel. A mist came down and they got hopelessly lost. It's just as well they were miles off course; if they'd fallen from the Crags they could have been killed. Three students died on the Crags last December. These lads were very lucky. They are also very fit and they'll be released from hospital tomorrow. They probably think it's a great adventure, the silly young sods. The Wallfield trip was well planned, and it's a pity the supervision broke down at the end of the holiday.'

Other news stories

You should note that in the following news stories — two based on statistical information and two based on biographical notes — you should apply the same criteria in terms of news values and news points, and the same techniques in terms of the intro, the news angle, and the over-all structures of the stories. Since the stories are for local newspapers you should lead with the most recent or important local news.

1 Walls and Dalesmoor Police have just released statistics for road accidents and driving offences in the past year. The figures in brackets are the equivalent numbers for the previous year.

Use the statistics below to write a news story of not more than 100 words for the Wallfield Mercury.

Figures for the year ending 31 December:

Total number of all recorded accidents involving one or more road vehicle: 217 (259)
Fatal accidents 17 (23)
Serious injuries: 101 (131)

Total number of all recorded accidents involving pedestrians: 63
(57)
Fatal accidents: 7 (4)
Serious injuries 34 (31)

Convictions for serious motoring offences, excluding drink-related offences: 47 (42)

Convictions for driving with more than the legal limit of alcohol: 51 (59)

2 Wallfield Chamber of Commerce have just released a survey of future trends in employment, sales and production among member firms in the Chamber of Commerce. Questionnaires were sent to 137 member firms, and 87 firms returned completed questionnaires.

The information below has been given to the Wallfield Mercury for publication in next week's issue. Write a news story of not more than 100 words.

Employment:
19 firms (21.8% of sample) said they expected to recruit more staff in the next six months;
18 firms (20.6% of sample) said they expected their staffing levels to remain the same;
50 firms (57.5% of sample) said they expected their staffing levels to fall in the next six months.

Sales and production:
20 firms (23% of sample) said they expected their sales or production to rise in the next six months;
23 firms (26.5% of sample) said they expected sales or production to remain at the same levels;
44 firms (50.5% of sample) said they expected their sales or production to fall in the next six months.

3 A Glasborough businessman has been awarded the OBE in the Queen's Birthday Honours List for services to the community.

Use the information below to write a news story of not more than 80 words for the Glasborough Gazette.

Mr Henry Warrender, aged 54, lives at 78 South Market Road, Glasborough, with his wife, Helena. Two children and two grandchildren. Educated at Glasborough High School. Began his career as apprentice quantity surveyor with Cairns & Pettigrew, Glasborough. Owns Warrender Timber Services, a firm he founded in Glasborough over 20 years ago, and employs 54 staff. From 1968 to 1974 was Independent councillor on former Glasborough Borough Council. In 1979 was a founder member of the Friends of Glasborough Hospice; chairman of Hospice fund-raising committee since 1982, raising over £55,000. Past chairman of Glasborough Rotary Club. Earlier this year re-elected president of Glasborough Chamber of Commerce — the only person to have held that office twice this century.

Mr Warrender said of the award: 'I am deeply honoured. I see the award as a tribute to the people of Glasborough as much as to me personally.'

4 The former headmaster of Glasborough High School died last week after a long illness.

Use the information below to write an obituary of not more than 100 words for the Glasborough Gazette.

Mr John Ashton was born in Glasborough in 1920. Educated at Glasborough High School and Durham University. Graduated with first class honours in physics in 1941. Worked on submarine radar systems for the War Ministry from 1941 to 1945. Completed a teacher training course at Durham in 1946. In the same year he was appointed a teacher of physics at King Edward's School, Wallfield. Appointed principal teacher of science at Glasborough High School in 1957; appointed head-master of Glasborough High School in 1966.

His main recreation was music. Conducted Wallfield's Centenary Choir from 1949 to 1957. Composed choral works for Glasborough Choral Society and conducted the Society's choirs until last year; appointed president of Choral Society in 1975. Was a founder member of Glasborough Arts Festival in 1965; appointed president of Arts Festival in 1978.

Mr Andrew Neave, headmaster of Glasborough High School, said: 'As a scholar and as a musician, John Ashton made an incalculable contribution to the quality of life in Glasborough. He will be deeply missed by his colleagues and many friends. We offer our deepest sympathy to his wife and his two sons.'

Exercises in intro writing

Re-write the intros overleaf in more effective ways.

1 No one was seriously injured when a coach with 38 holiday-makers was in collision with a lorry on the southern approach to Inverness yesterday.

2 According to a report published today, British men between the ages of 35 and 45 are healthier than ever before.

3 North Dale Crags, the popular tourist attraction in Dales-moor, was the scene of a tragedy last Saturday when a young rock climber, 18-year-old student Mark Wallister from Glas-borough, fell 150 ft to his death.

4 A memorial service will be held for Colonel Michael Forbes-Stuart who commanded the Durham Light Infantry in Durham Cathedral.

5 It has been suggested by Mrs Hazel Bush, secretary of the local ratepayers' association, that Glasborough District Council's hospitality budget is excessive.

6 At 11.30 pm on Saturday 15 November at Dempster's Disco in Albert Street, Wallfield, police were called to a disturbance as a result of which three men were arrested and one policeman was slightly injured.

7 A five-year sponsorship deal has been agreed by Wallfield businessman Charles Lawson and the chairman of Wallfield United Football Club which will save the 98-year-old club from bankruptcy.

8 Three youths are being sought by police who were seen by the building before the fire in Victoria Street, Wallfield.

9 Three youths are being held by police over the fire in Victoria Street, Wallfield.

10 As a consequence of new legislation which will become effective on 1 January a majority of married women in full-time employment will be required to contribute higher National Insurance payments.

11 Chaos erupted as Alliance, Conservative and Labour coun-cillors clashed furiously in last week's tempestuous meeting of the finance committee when Labour Leader Mr Trevor Armitage slammed the Conservative's bombshell move to axe sheltered housing and slash the leisure and recreation budget.

12 In a speech to members of the Glasborough Constituency Conservative Party last night Mr Wilfred Nugent said he would not contest the next general election.

13 Wallfield couple Henry and Joan Prescott hoped for a memorable holiday when they set off last month for a camping holiday in France but instead they experienced a holiday they would rather forget.

14 Councillor Harry Vaughan was seriously injured last Wednesday when his car, a two-year old white Ford Escort with beige upholstery, was in collision with a lorry at the entrance to Wallfield Industrial Estate.

15 Councillor Harry Vaughan, who suffered a broken pelvis and three cracked ribs in a road accident last month, is making a good recovery in Wallfield Infirmary where a new cardiac unit will be opened next month.

16 A Glasborough woman has been awarded first prize in a national painting competition.

17 After three years of intensive research at Glasborough University a team of scientists have developed a new treatment for diabetes.

18 When the local firm Wallfield Engineering Supplies Ltd closes this week, 375 people will be made redundant.

19 Legal action has been threatened by Councillor Clive Roberts, the highly respected chairman of Glasborough District Council's finance committee, against Mrs Hazel Bush, the controversial secretary of the local ratepayers' association.

20 Scientists and industrialists from throughout Britain will attend a three-day conference at Glasborough University next week to discuss the safety of the nuclear energy industry, the building programme for nuclear power stations over the next 20 years, the disposal of nuclear waste, the dangers of radiation, the long-term energy needs of the British economy, energy conservation, and alternative sources of energy.

4

INTERVIEWS

An interview is a dialogue which is arranged, planned and controlled by the interviewer for the specific purpose of gaining information for publication. An effective interview, unlike a conversation between equals, should be an uneven dialogue; the interview is directed by the interviewer but the interviewer should speak much less than the subject being interviewed.

Interviews

Personal interviews, either face-to-face or by telephone, are one of the main sources of news for any newspaper. Even when news is gained from other sources such as news releases or council meetings the news can be expanded and clarified by interviews with the persons involved. The art of interviewing is an essential professional skill for a reporter.

Planning

A journalist sometimes has no choice but to conduct an interview at such short notice that the dialogue has to be improvised. An improvised interview can sometimes be effective, but since it is unplanned and probably unstructured, it gives the interviewer little opportunity to direct the dialogue in an informed way. There is then a risk that the interview will be controlled and directed by the person being interviewed, the subject, rather than by the journalist, or that the dialogue will be a shapeless, faltering event that makes the journalist sound like a fumbling amateur rather than a skilled professional.

You will be at a serious disadvantage if you try to conduct an interview with a subject about whom you know nothing. An interview is more likely to be effective if it is planned and structured in advance. You should discover as much as you can about the person to be interviewed by using standard source books such as *Who's Who, Who's Who In Education, Who's Who In The Theatre*; you may be able to discover something about the subject's work, achievements and reputation from your newspaper's cuttings library, or by asking your editor or chief reporter.

Structure your interview by preparing a number of key questions in advance, but keep the structure simple and flexible so that you can follow up observations your subject makes during the interview.

For example, there would be an appropriate structure for an interview with a local councillor who had announced his decision to retire from politics after, say, 35 years in local government. You should begin by asking why he has decided to retire from politics, or how he reached his decision, and you would end by asking him how he intends to spend his free time. Between the first question and the last there would be several other key questions, so that the structure might be like this:

Why have you decided to retire from politics?
How, or when, did you reach your decision?
When did you first enter local politics?
What was it like to be in local government at that time?
Were you involved in any difficult election contests?
How do your early days compare with the present?
What are some of the main changes that have taken place during your political career?
What do you think of the relationship between local and central government?
What offices have you held in your 35 years in local government?
What do you think are your main achievements in that time?
Do you feel you have achieved all that you hoped to achieve?
Do you think the public appreciate or understand the work of local councillors?
Have you any regrets about those thirty-five years?
Have you any regrets about retiring now?
How do you intend to spend your free time now that you've retired?

Between one question and another you would of course

follow up any interesting leads your subject gave in his answers. A simple structure — in fact, a script — should be prepared for most interviews, and in some cases the script will be determined by the particular news angle you or your editor decide to follow. Further examples of structured interviews are given later in this chapter.

Protocol

In your own interests, in the interests of your newspaper, and in the interests of the subjects you interview you should observe a certain procedure for all interviews.

You should identify yourself and your newspaper before the dialogue begins. You should clearly inform your subject that you hope to get information which will be published in your newspaper, and that you hope this information will include quotes which can be attributed to the subject by name, age, occupation and address. Some people do not realise that the conversation they have with a journalist will lead to a published story, and they can be genuinely surprised and embarrassed to find their words — along with their name, age, address and occupation — printed in the local newspaper. If you fail to identify yourself or your newspaper, or if you fail to advise your subject that his actual words, and his name, age, occupation and address, may be published in a future edition of your newspaper, the subject could then protest that he was misled by you. Such a protest, even an ill-founded one, does nothing for your reputation or for the reputation of your newspaper.

Always try to have information fully on the record; that is, try to persuade your subject that the information he gives can be published and can be attributed to him by name. A fully attributed direct quote carries much more authority and human interest than reported speech in the third person. If the subject refuses this and resists your attempts to persuade him, you must then respect his wishes, but you should try to persuade him that the information, including quotes, should be published unattributed. If the subject refuses even this, ask him if he can give you the names of other persons who may be able to give you fully attributable information.

If your subject offers you information off the record — in

confidence and not for publication — accept it under those terms, but you may have to warn your subject that you may get the same information from another source, in which case the information will be published.

Never use active deception in an interview. It is not deception if a journalist witholds information from his subject, and it may be permissible for the journalist to imply that he already knows more about a story than he actually does, but it is ethically and sometimes legally wrong for the journalist to pretend that he is someone other than who he is. Deception is the method of the confidence trickster, not the professional journalist.

Similarly, never try to use coercion to gain information since this too is ethically and usually legally wrong. Information gained by deception or by threats can be denied later by a subject, and a public denial — even a false denial — could seriously damage your newspaper's reputation.

Never misquote your subject unless it is necessary. On some occasions it may be necessary to edit a quote in order to delete an obscenity or a libel. On other occasions it may be advisable to edit a clumsily ungrammatical quote which would expose your subject, and your newspaper, to ridicule. If it is necessary to edit a quote the editing must be done without changing your subject's meaning.

Interview techniques

Personal manner

The basis of a good interview technique is the interviewer's personal manner. This is not the same as personality. The personal manner you assume for an interview may consist entirely of acquired professional skills which conceal an unsuitable personality. A journalist whose normal personality is sullen and antagonistic should be capable of courtesy and persuasion when conducting an interview. The interview after all is not a natural, spontaneous conversation between equals but a one-sided dialogue which is arranged, planned and directed by the interviewer. Almost every interview — by personnel officers, doctors, police, and welfare workers as well as journalists — is a contrived situation in the sense that it is arranged and managed. The competent interviewer will make the contrivance socially acceptable, and the skilled interviewer will direct the dialogue in such a way that the subject is unaware of the contrivance.

Your manner should normally be positive, courteous, concerned, encouraging and persistent, and you should approach your subject in the belief that with this manner — applied to a planned, structured and controlled dialogue — you will get the information you need.

Be prepared to adapt your manner in special circumstances. For example, be sensitive to the fact that a bereaved family may be in a state of shock as well as grief when you try to interview them. An accident victim or the victim of an assault may also be in a state of shock, and as a result of the incident the victim could be confused about the simplest everyday realities.

Situations like these demand patience and sensitivity, qualities which are also needed when you interview the very young or the very old. Young children have such a small body of experience that they find if difficult, sometimes impossible, to organise and interpret new experience. Young children are also highly suggestible and may try to tell you what they think you want to hear. Elderly people, of course, can draw on a much greater volume of experience, and it is sometimes this store of experience that makes an older person seem slow to respond to questions. The old person's response seems delayed because he or she is considering a wide range of experience before giving a reply. What you should also remember about many old people is that their attitudes and their sense of values — social, political, and religious — may well have been formed and become entrenched before you were born.

Relationships

You should adapt your manner in special circumstances in order to meet the particular needs of the subject you are interviewing. The art of adaptation can also help you to gain the confidence of your subject and create the conditions for an effective interview.

As you approach the interview, try to suspend or neutralise

your personal attitudes, emotions and sense of values so that you can be more attentive to the attitudes, emotions and values of your subject. Even if you despise your subject's opinions and values you should not express open disagreement or disapproval except in extreme cases. If you express open disagreement — and the disagreement can be communicated by a change in your facial expression, your posture or your tone of voice — your subject is likely to become defensive. Defensiveness may make your subject more guarded in his disclosures or may even prompt him to end the interview. Defensiveness may prompt other subjects into angry exaggeration of their real point of view so that what should be a controlled dialogue can be reduced to a squabble in which facts and genuine viewpoints are lost in ludicrous overstatement. By expressing disagreement or disapproval you can ruin the interview.

An interview can also be ruined by your expression of embarrassment, and here again you should remember that your embarrassment can be communicated by something as simple as breaking eye-contact with your subject. If you communicate embarrassment your subject may feel that he has said or done something socially unacceptable, or that he himself is socially unacceptable. Your embarrassment will cost you your subject's confidence and it could bring the interview to an end.

How then does one avoid embarrassment? Embarrassment is a normal response to an incident which a person cannot assimilate, a response to a form of inadmissible emotional evidence that catches a person off guard and evokes an uncontrolled reaction — the nervous giggle or guffaw. But all evidence is admissible to a journalist; it becomes admissible and assimilable when it has been imagined, formed in the imagination.

You cannot anticipate everything that every subject will say or do, but you can accept that some of the people you meet will be eccentric, or grotesque, or criminal: they will have built models of all the Royal Palaces in spent matchsticks; they will have disfigured themselves through drink or drugs; they will have committed sexual abuse on their own children. The world includes such people, and you may have to interview

45

them. You will find it less difficult to accept these realities and to avoid expressing embarrassment or alarm during an interview if you remain interested in what your subject has to say, no matter how eccentric or grotesque or criminal the subject may be. Professional curiosity, exercised as part of the professional discipline of the controlled dialogue, will make embarrassment an irrelevant response.

The same professionalism should prevent your gratuitous laughter, which can ruin an interview even more certainly than an expression of embarrassment. A sudden burst of laughter will be like a slap in the face to someone who is genuinely trying to give a sincere response to your question. The subject will feel that he is the object of your ridicule and he will rightly be unwilling to expose himself to further ridicule; the interview will be over. To laugh **with** your subject is to strengthen the rapport, the working relationship which is essential for an effective interview; to laugh **at** your subject is to cancel the rapport.

A bad interview leaves the subject feeling cheated, diminished and unwilling to talk to you or your newspaper in the future. A good interview should normally leave the subject feeling that he has had a fair hearing and that he would be willing to speak to you again.

Practical techniques

Identities

Always observe the protocol outlined above. When you have identified yourself and your purpose you should offer some preliminary remarks such as: 'Thank you for agreeing to talk to me. It's good of you to give me your time', or 'I realise you must be busy and I'm grateful to you for sparing me the time. I'd be really glad to have your views (or advice or help) on this issue.' These introductory courtesies, as well as being a necessary social exchange, can help to establish a rapport between you and your subject.

You should then identify your subject by name, age, occupation and address. If you have any doubt about your subject's name or the name of his street ask him to spell out the names: William Gardener, Gardiner, Gardner or Garner of 213 Hutcheson Street, Hutchison Street or Hutchinson Street?

Full and precise identification is essential. It is not uncommon for a father and son living at the same address to have the same name. And in one and the same street there could be a William Gardener and a William Garner, or even two men with the same name, William Gardener, but it is hardly possible that there could be more than one William Gardener, aged 53, a hospital administrator living at 213 Hutcheson Street, Wallfield.

Before the interview begins, or as soon as possible after it has begun, you should know whether you are interviewing your subject as a means to some other end or if the subject is the end in himself. For example, if you interview someone who has witnessed an accident the main point of the interview of course is to get information about the accident; you will probably need little information about the witness apart from his identity. In contrast to this, if you are interviewing someone who has just been appointed chief officer of Glasborough District Council then the subject will be the whole point of the interview and you will want a great deal of personal, biographical information. You must direct the dialogue so that you get the information you need.

The dialogue

You will normally use a mix of specific, or closed, questions and general, or open, questions. A specific question is designed to elicit precise, factual information; a general question invites a statement of opinion.

For example, if you were interviewing the newly appointed chief officer of Glasborough District Council you would ask specific questions such as:

> How long have you worked as an official in local government?
> What was your first post?
> What other posts have you held in local government?

These specific questions invite precise, factual answers. In the same interview you would probably ask general questions such as:

> What do you think of the town of Glasborough?

How do you think the relationship between local and central government might develop in the next few years?

Try to avoid asking too many specific questions that can be answered simply by the words yes or no. A succession of yes/no questions will soon sound like an interrogation rather than a dialogue, and a succession of yes/no answers gives only the minimum of information. A more revealing dialogue will be achieved if a specific yes/no question is followed by a more general, open question. In the Glasborough District Council interview, for example, you could ask the newly appointed chief officer:

Will you move house to Glasborough? (specific)
What do you think about the environment in and around Glasborough? (general)

A succession of Why? questions, like a succession of specific yes/no questions, can soon sound like an interrogation. Why? questions can be useful in establishing the reason for an action or a case of cause and effect:

Why was a fifth-form pupil suspended from Glasborough High School?
Why was Hutcheson Street closed to traffic on Wednesday morning?
Why did the workers at a Wallfield engineering firm go on strike last week?

But too often the Why? question is used where no reason can be given and where there is no case of cause and effect; on some occasions the Why? question is unanswerable in the form in which it is asked:

Why do you enjoy angling as a recreation?
Why did you design your garden in that way?
Why do you breed Siamese cats?

These questions cannot be answered in terms of cause and effect, or in terms of a logical reason. They are really questions about motive but since few of us are clearly aware of our motives or willing to reveal them the three questions are unnecessarily difficult. The most appropriate answer to each of these questions would be that the activity referred to meets some emotional need which is ultimately inexplicable. It would be more productive to re-phrase the three questions like this:

What are some of the things you enjoy about angling? or: Do you go angling simply to catch fish or is there more to it than that?
How did you arrive at that design for your garden? Did it involve a great deal of work?
When did you begin to breed Siamese cats?

As the interview proceeds use a simple repertoire of sounds and signs to signal encouragement and reassurance to your subject. The repertoire could consist of remarks like 'Yes', 'I see', 'Really?' 'Uhuh' and 'Mm', along with nods and smiles. These signals tell the subject that you are listening, you are interested, and that you understand or want to understand what he is saying. Your encouragement and reassurance will help to maintain rapport throughout the interview and persuade the subject to respond in a positive way.

Your repertoire of signals can help to break a silence and encourage your subject to proceed after a slight pause. Try to be aware of the significance of a pause. If the subject is considering his answer then all you need do is nod or say 'Yes' and wait for the answer, but if the subject has completed his answer — or seems to think he has completed it — then you should proceed to your next question.

A subject will sometimes hesitate after making a particularly emphatic statement, as if he felt he had revealed too much or gone too far. What you should then do is echo the subject's statement in your own words. For example, if your subject said:

All our councillors are useless! Bloody useless!

you should say:

You think none of them do a good job.

If your subject said:

I've been passed over for promotion five times.
Top management must have it in for me.

you should say:

You think you're being treated unfairly.

If your words are spoken in a sympathetic or at least neutral tone, and spoken as a statement rather than a question, the effect is to prompt your subject to think again and offer a more considered — usually a more accurate or truly representative — answer. When you bridge this kind of silence in the right way the interview sometimes moves on in a new direction that reveals more information.

Be very cautious about using the 'pregnant pause'. If you make deliberate use of silences the effect could be to break the continuity of the dialogue and disconcert the subject, who may feel that you are trying to play a cat and mouse game. He might then become suspicious and reluctant to volunteer information.

Non-verbal communication

Try to interpret your subject's non-verbal communication, or body language, in the course of the interview, and try to be aware of the extent to which the non-verbal communication (NVC) confirms or contradicts your subject's spoken communication.

NVC should be interpreted with caution because it may not convey precise meanings. Your subject's posture, use of gesture, and even facial expressions may simply be his habitual manner to which no special significance can be attached. Even so, certain aspects of NVC are worth noting.

A closed posture sometimes reveals anxiety or tension. If your subject is sitting in a hunched, forward-leaning posture with his legs together, his arms close to his body and his hands clasped or clenched then he may be nervous. In contrast, if he is leaning back in his chair with his legs stretched out in an open sprawl then he is probably relaxed.

Your subject's spoken answers may be accompanied by a pattern of gestures which will normally reinforce the answers he gives. Note the extent to which your subject's words are confirmed by the movements of his arms, hands and fingers, the shrugging of shoulders, and the nodding or shaking of his head.

Facial expression can be revealing, and the general significance of a smile or frown is usually obvious. You should also try to be aware of the constantly changing tensions in your subject's face, the face beneath the face that may indicate a change of mood or an uncertainty, or a particular expression — wistful, ironic, troubled, amused — that suggests your subject is thinking of associated ideas or experiencing emotions that he may not be expressing in words. If you see a shift of facial expression at a significant point in the interview, especially if the shift is followed by a pause, then you should gently intervene with a question like 'How do you feel about that?' or 'How do you think this came about?' or 'What do you think about these things?'

Your interview should always involve eye-contact between you and your subject. Any personal encounter that involves no eye-contact whatsoever is usually felt to be incomplete, and one or more of the persons in the encounter may feel that they have not received the simple human recognition that is an important part of any human relationship, even the functional relationship of a press interview. But continuous eye-contact — except between lovers or people engaged in angry confrontation — is normally oppressive. Your subject may feel that he is being scrutinised or stared down in a conflict of wills if you make prolonged eye-contact with him. You should normally meet your subject's eye as you ask your questions and hold eye-contact during part of his answers.

Telephone interviews

The majority of press interviews are conducted by telephone. They follow the same procedure as face-to-face interviews and you should observe the same protocol, assume the same manner and apply the same techniques. The obvious difference between telephone interviews and face-to-face meetings is that non-verbal communication is possible only in personal encounters. But useful supplementary information can be gained from a telephone interview if you listen intelligently.

As soon as your subject begins to speak you can normally detect if the subject is male or female, young or old; you will also hear whether the subject speaks in a regional accent or in received pronunciation (an 'educated' accent, or 'BBC English'), which can give some indication of social class.

Note your subject's tone of voice, volume and pace, and try

to be aware of any changes in these — sometimes known as paralinguistic factors — during the interview. It is impossible to attach precise meanings to these changes, but there could be a connection between a question you ask and a hardening or softening in your subject's tone of voice, a quickening of pace or a falling away without completing an answer, or an awkward pause.

Encourage and reassure your subject on the telephone by using the same simple repertoire of signals, including smiles and nods of the head; although they cannot be seen the smiles and nods can have the effect of reinforcing the tone of approval in your voice.

You must be able to conduct a telephone interview in such a way that you gain all the information you need, but the telephone interview by its very nature can never be as revealing as the face-to-face interview. When you have the choice of one or the other you should always opt for the personal encounter rather than a dialogue of disembodied voices.

> This chapter has so far discussed the press interview in terms of a controlled dialogue between a journalist and a subject, but there can be occasions when your subject presents you with problems which make it difficult to establish a dialogue. This section offers a number of techniques that may help you to solve the more common problems.

Problem interviews

The 'Don't Knows'

Almost every political opinion poll and social survey has a percentage of 'Don't Knows', and almost every reporter experiences occasions when a subject agrees to be interviewed and then responds to a succession of questions with replies like 'I don't know', 'I'm not sure', 'I'll have to think about that', or 'Now you're asking'. If it becomes clear that the subject genuinely does not know and has no information to offer, then you should bring the interview politely to a close. But if you think the subject has something valid to say then you should persist with the interview and develop a dialogue by prompting your subject. The prompting must be done with great care and patience so that you do not hurry the subject into giving you the answers he thinks you want, in which case the interview would be fiction. Skilful prompting, by offering the subject realistic options, can be effective.

Every week for several years this writer met the winner of a newspaper's spot the ball competition. When the inevitable question: 'What will you do with the money?' was asked it sometimes produced the answer: 'I don't know. I'll have to think about it.' If the interview had ended there the news editor and the competitions manager would have been understandably angry, and the competition winner might have been disappointed if their newspaper had treated them with so little concern. A simple repertoire of realistic prompts usually produced a positive response.

Depending on the time of year, and the identity and circumstances of the winner of the competition, the prompts were:

> Have you booked a holiday this year? What difference will the prize money make to your holiday?
> Have you bought your Christmas presents? Will you be buying any more now that you've won Spot the Ball?
> Your husband/wife will probably have ideas about how to spend the money. How do you think they would like to spend it?
> Do you have children/grandchildren? Will you use some of the prize money for them? What would they like?
> Will you have a night out to celebrate your win?
> What kind of night would you like?
> Wouldn't you like to treat yourself or your husband/wife to something really different?

This kind of prompting is sometimes necessary when you interview people who suddenly find themselves in totally new roles or undergoing new experiences. (For many of your subjects the press interview itself will be a new experience). In circumstances like these even highly articulate people can find themselves momentarily speechless. But the circumstances will often be predictable; you will know before some interviews take place that your subjects may be at a loss for words, and you should include some prompts as you plan and structure these interviews. As you begin to establish the dialogue of the interview you should prompt your subjects by helping them to interpret the new experience, relating it to past experience in their own lives or comparing it with experience in the lives of friends, relatives or neighbours. You should also persuade them to try their new role, to think their way into it and then tell you how it feels.

'No comment'

The second of our problem interviews presents us with a subject who is less open to persuasion than the Don't Know. A good story can be lost if the person who is centrally involved refuses to be interviewed.

The refusal is sometimes the unconsidered response, an almost reflex action of a person who has never dealt with the press and for whom an interview, especially a telephone interview, seems an intrusive or troublesome event. Such a person may be persuaded if your manner is reassuring and politely persistent. A realistic example is one in which a middle-aged couple object to a planning application which would affect their immediate environment. Your telephone approach might be this:

Q Good morning. Mr Wrightson?
A Yes.
Q This is the Glasborough Gazette. My name is Napier and I . . .
A I can't talk to the press.
Q I see. I was hoping you could advise me about the planning application for Wellside Gardens. It'll only take a minute.
A No. I'm sorry. No.
Q It's really quite straightforward, Mr Wrightson, and quite simple. I mean, it's understandable that you would object to an application like that, isn't it?
A Is it?
Q Yes. A building like that could affect your environment, couldn't it? It's understandable that someone in your position should object to the application.
A My position?

Q Well, yes. The proposed building would be next door to you, wouldn't it?
A It would. Yes.
Q How close would it be, Mr Wrightson? A few yards?
A Yes. Just two or three yards.
Q And the proposal is for a four-storey block of flats?
A Four? No, it's six storeys. It'll block out the light, you see.
Q I see. And how will it affect the immediate environment?
A Well, the thing would dominate the whole street. In fact, it would dominate all the surrounding streets. There's nothing more than three storeys in this area at the moment.

And the dialogue has begun. The reporter can now go on to ask the subject to discuss his objections in more detail, or to ask how the new building might affect the value of his house and other houses in the immediate area.

Other, more stubbornly resistant subjects may not be persuaded by your reassuring manner, and on these occasions your approach should be a tactical one. A useful tactic is to speak as if you knew more than you actually did; you could even imply that you already have the story and simply want a comment from the subject. You should also suggest that it is in the subject's own best interests to offer a comment.

If we take the example of the planning application and consider a telephone interview with the applicant, the managing director of a building company, your approach could be something like this:

Q Good morning, Mr Sheldon. I'm calling from the Glasborough Gazette. My name is Napier.
A No comment.
Q I'll be very grateful for a minute or two of your time and I . . .
A I told you, no comment.
Q We're publishing a story about your planning application for Wellside Gardens and we'd be glad to have your views.
(Silence)
Q Glasborough people will be interested in your proposal for Wellside Gardens. Do you think your application will be approved?
(Silence)
Q We've spoken to the other interested parties, of course, and

we'd like to complete the picture. We really would like to hear your views on this.

A Not today, thank you.

Q It would be a pity if your side of the case went by default. That would affect your application, couldn't it?

A What do you mean?

Q Well, we've spoken to the people in Wellside Gardens and to the local councillor. If we publish only their side of the argument next week it could influence the planning committee.

A What are these people saying about it?

Q They seem to have some very detailed objections. We feel you should have this chance to put your side of the argument. (Silence)

Q Don't you think your associates in the company, and your employees, will be disappointed if they don't read your side of the argument next week?

A They know where we stand.

Q But they'll want to see you defend the company's position. And the planning committee will too.

A What do you mean?

Q Well, I have to say it will look unfortunate if our story gives details of the objections but no comment from you. I mean, it's a straightforward application, isn't it?

A Of course it's straightforward.

Q And there is a need for housing in that area, isn't there, Mr Sheldon?

A Yes. And that's one of the very few vacant sites.

Q How soon could work start once you get planning permission?

A We could start in a matter of days.

Q And how long would building work last?

A Eight months. Yes, about eight months.

And at last a dialogue has begun. The reporter could go on to ask about the interior fittings of the flats, the external appearance, the price range, and the likely demand from buyers.

If Mr Sheldon had adamantly refused to comment the reporter should have ended the interview politely and then he should have telephoned the company again and asked to speak to a different person — the sales manager or works manager — in an attempt to get a comment. If, despite the reporter's efforts to get both sides of the argument, the company had still refused to comment, the reporter should have written the story with the available information, making it clear that the company had declined the opportunity to comment.

Victims and families

Sensitivity must be shown when you interview the victims of accidents or assaults, or the families of the victims, and an even more delicate approach is essential when you interview a bereaved family. Local newspapers, involved as they are in the lives of communities and observing human values as well as news values, deal more humanely with these situations than some sections of the national press. A measure of the local newspaper's humanity is the editor's willingness to forego an interview rather than cause additional distress to victims and families.

The normal recommendation of polite persistence in dealing with reluctant subjects does not apply to victims of accidents or assaults or to the families of the dead. The victims may be in a state of shock or acute anxiety, in which case persistent questioning against their wishes will delay their recovery. Similarly, persistent, unwelcome questioning of bereaved families will prolong and perhaps intensify their distress. The health of the victim and the dignity of the bereaved family are more important than the interview.

A possible approach to a victim, once you have identified yourself, is this:

> I'm sorry to hear of your accident. It must have been quite an ordeal. How do you feel now?

If the victim is still unwell you may ask:

> Would you like to tell me about the incident? No? Do you think you'll be able to tell me about it later?

If the victim is unwilling you should offer your hopes for his speedy recovery and bring the meeting to an end. Information about the incident may be available from the police, or from relatives, neighbours, friends or colleagues of the victim.

A possible approach to a bereaved family is this:

> I'm sorry to hear of your terrible loss. I understand how difficult a time this is for you. Is there some way the Gazette can help?

Would it help if you told me something about your husband/
wife/son/daughter?
Would you like to talk?
Do you think you would be able to talk to me later?

If the bereaved family say no, you should offer your sympathy
and then leave. Here again it should be possible to get
information from other sources — from relatives, neighbours
or friends, or from the police, fire service or hospital.

> Every interview is unique because the subject — the
> person being interviewed — is unique, but there are
> certain recurring events and situations for which the
> same basic interview structure can be used. Some of
> these events, along with checklists of questions, are
> outlined here.

Interview Checklists

Fires

The main concern here is human life; other concerns are the
damage to property, and the cause and extent of the fire. Your
sources of information will be: the victims of the fire if they
are fit to be interviewed, eye-witnesses, fire service, police,
hospital. Your questions should include the following:

Was anyone injured?
If so, how many people?
Names, ages, occupations and addresses of the injured?
The nature of the injuries?
Have the injured received medical attention?
Was anyone taken to hospital?
Was anyone else involved? Eye-witnesses?
How did the people get out of the building?
Who discovered the fire or raised the alarm?
When was the fire discovered?
What was the cause?
How many fireman and appliances attended?
How long did it take to extinguish the fire?/Get the fire under
control?

What is the damage to the building and its contents?
Is the building structurally safe?
What is the estimated cost of the damage?
Was the building/were the contents insured?

Accidents

Once again the main concern here is human life. Your sources of information will be the same as your information sources for a fire: the victims, if they are fit to be interviewed, eye-witnesses, police, hospital and perhaps the fire service. Your questions should include:

Was anyone injured?
If so, how many people?
Names, ages, occupations and addresses of the injured?
The nature of the injuries?
Have the injured received medical attention?
Has anyone been taken to hospital?
Were other people involved in the incident but not injured? Eye-witnesses?

In the case of a road accident you should additionally ask:

How many vehicles were involved?
What types of vehicle?
Note the exact location of the accident.
Note the time of day and the weather conditions.

You must avoid implying responsibility in a road accident: your news story can state that vehicle A was in collision with vehicle B, but not that vehicle A collided with B.

Prize winners

Your main concern here is the identity of the winner and the nature of the prize. Your sources of information will be the winner and the organisers of the competition. Your questions should include:

Name, age, occupation and address of the prize-winner?
What does the prize consist of? If cash, how big a sum?
How will you use the money?
How do you feel about winning the prize?
Did you think you could win?

If the prize is for achievement, as in sport, entertainment or the arts, you should ask the winner:

> How long have you been active in the sport?
> What other distinctions have you achieved in the sport?
> Have you entered, and won, other competitions in the past? If so, what, and when?
> What are your hopes for your future in the sport?

If the prize is for a game of chance, such as football pools or spot the ball, you should ask the winner:

> How long have you been trying the game?/ How many times have you tried before this?
> Have you ever won before?
> If so, when, and what was the prize?
> Do you have a special system for playing the game?
> If so, can you tell me about it?
> Will you try the game again?

New schemes or projects

Your main concerns will be the project itself, the people for whom it is intended, and the director or originator of the project. Your main source of information will be the organisers of the project. Your questions should include:

> What exactly is the new project?
> What is the purpose or intention behind it?
> Whose idea was it?
> Who is it aimed at?
> How will it affect the people it is aimed at?
> Why is the project being launched now?
> How long will it run?
> What is the cost of the project?
> How is it being funded?
> Who will control/direct the project?
> How many other people will be involved in running it?

You could then follow up this interview by interviewing the director or the originator of the project.

New buildings

Your concerns here will be the nature of the building, its future owner or occupants, and perhaps its impact — architectural or commercial — on the environment. Sources of information include the building contractor, the architect, the owner or future occupant, the council planning department, persons who objected to the application. Your questions should include:

Where exactly is the building being built?
For what purpose?
Who will be the owner or occupants? Fully identify the owner or main occupant.
How will they use the new building?
Who is the builder/architect?
What is the cost of the building?
How is it being funded?
How long will building work last?
How many people will be employed in the construction stage?
What impact will the building/business have on the existing environment?
When were the plans passed?
Did anyone object to the planning application?
Is there a drawing or a plan I can use for publication in the next issue of the Gazette?

This interview could be followed by an interview with the owner, or future owner. If people objected to the planning application they could be interviewed.

New appointments

The main concern here is the identity of the person appointed to the post, and he or she will be your main source of information. Your questions should include:

Name, age, address and present/previous post of the newly appointed person?
What will your new job involve?/What are your responsibilities in your new post?
How many people will you be responsible for?
Will you be in control of a budget? If so, how big a budget?
How big a challenge will this be?
How do you feel about that?
What was your job immediately before this?
How do you think that job will compare with the new one?
What other posts have you held?

Where did you do your training?/Where were you educated?
How do you think the job might develop in the next few years?

Interview Exercises

1 A woman in your newspaper's circulation area has won a major prize on the football pools. What preliminary remarks would you make at the start of the interview, and what 10 questions would you ask her?

2 A Glasborough firm has won the Queen's Award for Industry. When you telephone the managing director to interview him for the Glasborough Gazette he claims he is too busy to talk to you. How would you persuade him to be interviewed? What 10 questions would you then ask?

3 Wallfield United football club dismiss the manager. He agrees to be interviewed by you for the Wallfield Mercury. What preliminary remarks would you make, and what questions would you ask?

4 The football club announce the appointment of a new manager and invite you to interview him in the presence of the club chairman. What questions would you ask the manager, and what questions would you ask the chairman?

5 A sixth-form pupil at Glasborough High School has won a national poetry prize but is reluctant to talk to the Gazette. How would you persuade her? What would you ask her in an interview?

6 The district council decide to stop funding a youth club in an area of youth unemployment. Who would you interview and what would you ask?

7 A local councillor telephones your editor protesting that he and his party have been under-reported in recent weeks. The councillor demands to be interviewed and your editor asks you to meet the councillor. What preliminary remarks would you make at the meeting? What questions would you ask?

8 The district council finally approve a planning application for a six-storey block of flats despite strong local objections.

Who would you interview in covering this story? How would you adapt your approach or your tactics for the different persons you would interview? What would you ask?

9 An elderly couple who live in your circulation area were on a European tour when their coach crashed in France. The man was uninjured but his wife suffered slight cuts. Three people on the coach were killed. The couple chose to return home after the accident rather than complete the tour in a replacement coach. How would you approach the interview? What questions would you ask?

10 A seven-year-old girl who was abducted on her way to school is found safe and well the same day and is re-united with her parents. No one has been charged with the offence. You call at the child's home for an interview. What preliminary remarks would you make? In what circumstances would you decide not to proceed with the interview, and what alternative source of information could you use? In what circumstances would you speak to the child, and what would you ask her? What would you ask the parents?

Additional exercises in interviewing are included in the multiple-task questions in Chapter 10.

5

STANDARD AND NON-STANDARD ENGLISH

The news story in the local weekly press and the broadsheet press is written in Standard English, the internationally agreed version of formal written English. The standardisation of written English was achieved through the acceptance of a number of conventions about the forms of words, sentences and paragraphs, and the standard will be maintained as long as the conventions are observed. Journalists have a vital role to play in maintaining the quality of written English, but in order to fulfil that role they must have a confident understanding of the conventions.

Standard and Non-Standard English

Standard English is the formal, written version of the English language. It is the language of textbooks, histories and biographies, of party political manifestos and of the reports of government departments, companies and committees of enquiry. Apart from fiction, almost all published work in continuous prose form is written in Standard English. The version of Standard English used in news writing is slightly modified in the sense that it normally avoids specialist diction, long, elaborate sentences and paragraphs, and stylistic mannerisms, as the next chapter, 'Prose style', will show.

The term, Standard English, simply indicates that this version of the language is a measure or criterion, a point of reference or comparison for all other versions of English.

In Standard English there is broad agreement about most linguistic features: sentence structures, punctuation, syntax, grammar and vocabulary. And since this agreement is internationally accepted the reader of *The Times* of London is able to read the Glasgow *Evening Times*, the Dublin *Irish Times*, the *New York Times*, the *Times of India* and the *Straits Times* of Singapore.

This degree of international recognition would be impossible without an agreed standard version of the language. Even in a single nation there would be no general understanding of the written word unless there were a standard form of the language; for example, the written dialect of Cumbria or West Central Scotland would be unintelligible to many British readers, as examples later in this chapter will show.

Non-Standard English in written form is any version of English that does not observe the standard agreement about sentence structures, punctuation, syntax, grammar and vocabulary.

Although Non-Standard English exists mainly in spoken form — slang, colloquialism, regional or national dialect — examples of written Non-Standard English can of course be found in the published texts of plays and in passages of dialogue in novels and short stories where the characters may speak in a casual, unstructured way, or in slang or regional dialect. Written Non-Standard English can also be found in advertising copywriting and in some 'popular' tabloid newspapers.

The fact that Standard English is so widely recognised and so widely used has led to the mistaken view that it is better or more correct than Non-Standard English, and even to the belief that Standard English is the only correct version of the language. This belief arose because Standard English was originally the language of a literate elite and has for centuries been the language of government and law, of religion and education — in other words, the language of authority. But in a literate nation like Britain Standard English is also the language of the people. Although it is more formal and systematic than most other versions of the language, Standard English as a means of communication is no better and no more correct than Non-Standard forms. Regional dialect English is spoken by millions of people in Britain, and national dialect English is spoken by hundreds of millions of people throughout the world. It is pointless to claim that these people are speaking the wrong language.

A more helpful approach is to think of versions of the English language in terms of their usefulness or appropriateness in particular human situations rather than their 'correctness'.

Regional dialect adequately expresses most of the language needs of most of the people of Britain most of the time, but dialects are not always understood outside their own region. Similarly, slang is often more vividly expressive than Standard English, but it is seldom as intelligible, partly because slang is not one single form of the language but many forms. Slang is used more by men than by women, and it is sometimes strongly associated with particular social, regional or occupational groups. Slang is also a highly volatile version of the language, so volatile that the slang of one generation — 'Wizard prang, old boy. What?' — is the archaism of the next. And there are always people who feel offended by slang.

Because Standard English is understood and accepted by all readers, irrespective of region, occupation or social class, it is the only effective version of the language for journalism.

Within Standard English itself there are ideas of what is acceptable and 'correct', as outlined in the second paragraph of this chapter. If these standards are not observed by the journalist then his version of the language may fluctuate uneasily between Standard and Non-Standard English. A news story in which the language changed from Standard to Non-Standard English would be unacceptable because it would draw attention to the writer's inconsistent technique rather than directing the reader's attention to the meaning of the story.

Non-Standard English

So far this statement has been written in Standard English, observing the conventions for sentence structures, punctuation, syntax, grammar and vocabulary. The following examples observe different conventions and are versions of Non-Standard English.

Sentence structures

A Standard English sentence is a complete unit of communication — a complete statement, or question, or command — in which the basic grammatical requirement is a finite verb, that is, a verb with a subject.

Ten days in sunny Spain for only £150.
Wallfield businessman guilty of £20,000 VAT fraud.
Penalty winner after last-minute goal-mouth scramble.

These three statements are effective communications but since none of them has a verb they are technically incomplete and therefore examples of Non-Standard English. They could, of course, be acceptable as headlines or picture captions in some newspapers.

Vocabulary

You want to get the old nut down, mate, and have a nice kip.
The old windbag got up on his hind legs and I knew he would rabbit on till the cows came home.
The bookies got the jitters and the punters got the lolly when the favourite romped home.

These three statements, all of them complete sentences, make their points through slang and are clearly Non-Standard English.

The following three statements, all in national or regional dialect English, are also forms of Non-Standard English:

Him bawlin' all de time 'nough fe wake de dead. (All the time he [was] bawling loud enough to wake the dead. West Indian English)
He's oop rake behint intek wi' tethera yows. (He is up the fell track behind the enclosure with three ewes. Cumbrian English)
Yon wee scunner aye gets in a stramash when he's bevvied. (That disgusting little person always gets into conflict when he has been drinking. Scots English)

Syntax

There can be regional or national variations in syntax, the word order in sentences:

Dead he was, boyo, I tell you. (Welsh)
Sure, amn't I just after telling you? (Irish)
What like is the weather, Jimmy? Are you for the gemme, but? (Scots)

67

Grammar

There is a colloquial grammar, much of it with regional associations, that runs parallel to the formal grammar of Standard English:

> You was the one what done it, wasn't you?
> Me? I ain't done nothing. Honest, I ain't.
> Them lads is telling me it were you.

Regional dialects, colloquialism and slang help to give the English language a diversity and vitality, but apart from the occasions when these diverse elements may appear as direct quotations, they have no place in the news story because they may not be understood by all readers, even within the limited circulation area of a local weekly newspaper. Standard English, on the other hand, is a world language and is understood by virtually everyone who is literate in English.

6

PROSE STYLE

A reporter's ability to write an accurate, intelligible news story is largely determined by his command of prose style. This chapter discusses the elements of prose style and shows how these elements should be applied in effective news writing.

Prose style

Prose style is sometimes referred to as if it were a mystery but a writer should regard prose style as a combination of skills, techniques, and attitudes — in other words, a craft — that can be acquired and developed.

The main elements of prose style can be identified as: diction or register, that is, the selection or range of words used in a piece of writing; sentence structures and paragraph structures; punctuation schemes; rhythm; and tone.

Diction or register

Diction or register is the choice of words in a given piece of writing or in speech. A word like 'diction' or 'register' is useful; there could be some confusion in referring simply to the 'language' of a passage of writing since language includes several features — for example, grammar, syntax and punctuation — as well as words. This concept of diction implies that there are ranges of words appropriate to particular subjects and contexts. If we take extreme examples, we find that the words in a legal document such as a will or a warranty have a different range from the words of an instruction manual on word processing. And in one and the same edition of a newspaper there will be obvious differences in the diction of various stories. The range of words used to report the opening of a new bypass road will differ from the range used to report a road accident; the weekly livestock market report will differ from the football report; the entertainments page, the cookery column, the book reviews will all use different ranges of words:

> Two first-half goals by Glasburgh Rovers dashed Wallfield's hopes for the league title.

and

> Prices fell sharply at Deanvale last week. Cattle were down to 91.5p a kg (−3.5p from last week) and sheep dropped 15.4p to 180.6p.

and

> Beechmount Players' Christmas revue, 'The Icing on the Cake', had the audience helpless with laughter on opening night last Saturday.

and

> Three Wallfield children were seriously injured on Monday when their school bus overturned on the Wallside bypass road.

Although diction is essentially a matter of words there are occasions when diction is reinforced by other linguistic features.

If once again we consider the example of a legal document we find such features as extended sentences with several clauses; repetition or repetition with only minor variations of some clauses, phrases and single words; a higher than normal use of upper case spellings; and the deliberate repetition of nouns in order to avoid the ambiguity of pronouns:

> The Company hereby GUARANTEES AND WARRANTS that save as provided in the said Conditions and in this Guarantee, in the event of the person entitled to the benefit of this Guarantee (hereinafter included in the term 'Client') notifying the Company in writing within a period of TWENTY YEARS from the date of completion of the work. . . .

Diction also depends to some extent on the journalist's personal command of vocabulary, a word range that is sometimes known as 'idiolect'. A journalist with a limited personal vocabulary could still be an effective writer, but such a journalist could find himself being assigned to a limited range of stories, or being treated not as a complete reporter but as a news-gatherer whose notes are re-written by a sub-editor. But no local newspaper can afford a journalist who cannot deliver finished copy.

Important features of diction which will significantly affect a writer's prose style are the differences between concrete and abstract, between monosyllabic and polysyllabic, and between neutral and emotive.

Concrete and abstract diction

concrete	abstract
people	the public/the population/the populace
neighbours	the community
voters	the electorate/constituents
newspapers	the press/news media
school/college	educational institution
shops	retail outlets
playing fields	outdoor recreational facilities

Apart from specialised terminologies in subject areas such as science, technology and medicine, concrete words are usually shorter than abstract words, and this simple difference in the length of words, especially the difference between words of one syllable and words of many syllables, will affect your prose style.

Monosyllabic and polysyllabic diction

monosyllabic	polysyllabic
work	employment/occupation
pay	remuneration
play	recreation
car	automobile
train	railway locomotive
small/slight	insubstantial/insignificant
meet	encounter/rendezvous with
prove	verify/corroborate/ascertain
think	reflect/cogitate/ratiocinate

Neutral and emotive diction

A journalist should try always to be aware of the difference between neutral diction and emotive diction. Neutral diction is the use of words in an impartial and objective way. Although the ideal of total impartiality and objectivity is almost impossible to attain it is an ideal the journalist should aim for in almost every story.

Emotive diction — words which tend to arouse an emotion in the mind of the reader — can be the result of the journalist failing to control his own emotions or failing to control his choice of words in a story. An occasional failure of control is understandable because it is impossible for a writer to be in total command of his emotions at all times, and impossible too for anyone to be in total control of the 400,000 to 500,000 words and variants in the English language. Even so, a journalist's involuntary use of emotive diction soon becomes tiresome for the sub-editor who has to re-write the copy, and if the unedited copy gets into print the story could be equally tiresome for the readers who want news of life in their villages, their towns, their cities, and not the emotional spasms of a young reporter.

You should always try to be aware of your sympathies and prejudices — in politics, on questions of nationality and race, in controversial social issues, and even in sport — and you should then control these sympathies and prejudices rather than be controlled by them.

An obvious example of emotive diction is to describe people waging guerilla warfare as 'gallant freedom fighters' or, from the opposite viewpoint, as 'terrorists' or 'bloody murderers'.

Other examples of emotive diction appear in press reports of local and national politics where opponents are said to 'launch furious attacks' on each other when they engage in political argument, and where a party is said to 'demolish' the opposition when that party wins a debate, or when the reporter claims the party has won the debate.

The partisan football reporter notes the 'vicious fouls' of the opposing team in contrast to the 'foolhardy' or 'despairing' fouls of the team he supports. And a win by the favoured team is a 'victory', or a 'triumph', or a 'triumphant victory' while a defeat — often the result of 'fate' or 'a blatantly offside goal' and 'wildly inconsistent refereeing' — is reported as a 'tragedy'.

An obvious effect of this kind of diction is that it inflates the currency of language: the writer selects words that give a heightened and sometimes spurious importance to the story. If everyday events are reported in this way then unusual events will need a further intensification of diction, but if a word like 'tragedy' has already been used to report a defeat in a football match, or words like 'inferno', 'conflagration' or 'holocaust' used to describe an unexceptional fire, then these words will not have enough impact to report genuinely tragic events such as the loss of human life. By inflating the currency of the language the reporter quickly reaches a state of linguistic bankruptcy; he runs out of words which will adequately record major events, and the newspaper must then try to make its impact visually rather than linguistically by using bigger and bigger headlines. This is the practice of the tabloid press where the impact of the news sometimes depends on the skill of the graphic artist as much as that of the reporter and the photographer, but it is not normally acceptable to the readers of a local newspaper who expect the life of their community to be reported in words and pictures rather than visual effects.

The difference between neutral and emotive diction is sometimes also a difference between fact and opinion as well as fact and hyperbole; the writer can use words with strong connotations so that the story has an inbuilt interpretation:

neutral	emotive
complain	bleat/gripe/moan
criticise	attack/blast/lash/slam
cut	axe/butcher/chop/slash
fall	crash/plummet/plunge/slump
rise	rocket/soar/spiral
private	clandestine/secret
unusual	bizarre/fantastic/mysterious
competitor	enemy/opponent/rival
friend	crony
explanation	cover-up/excuse/whitewash

There will be times when it will be right to use emotive words in a story. The fireman who enters a blazing house to bring out a young child deserves to be described as brave or heroic; the woman who spends several hours each week raising funds for the local hospice deserves to be called compassionate or public spirited; a youth convicted of a violent and unprovoked

73

assault on an elderly man can rightly be called a cowardly thug.

Even in cases like these it is better to let the facts speak for themselves. And the journalist should certainly avoid the wilful use of emotive words in a deliberate attempt to manipulate the emotions or opinions of the reader. A conscious attempt at emotional manipulation will almost inevitably distort the facts of a story. At the same time the attempt would betray the readers' trust, and when a newspaper betrays its readers' trust then it loses that trust and may also lose some readers.

This kind of manipulative writing can be found in the tabloid 'popular' press where some political stories are written in such crudely partisan terms, and human stories in such crassly sentimental terms, that the writing mixes fact and emotion to the extent that the stories cease to be news and become that distinctive genre, tabloid fantasy.

These different dictions will produce different effects in the journalist's prose style.

If a news story has a high frequency of concrete, monosyllabic words then the diction will tend to be highly specific and the story will almost certainly refer to primary, physical realities — people and places, actions and incidents, sharply defined detail. And if the diction is contained within short, simply structured sentences, then the prose style will be terse and brisk. This kind of writing often has a forceful simplicity, a directness and immediacy that can make a strong impact on the reader: the clear presentation of names and places, of incidents and details in a firmly constructed narrative framework is the essence of good news writing.

By contrast, it is seldom acceptable in news writing to use a heavy concentration of abstract, polysyllabic words. Such diction would refer to ideas, concepts and theories rather than people, places and objects; it would be remote from the physical realities of life and therefore remote from the experience, or at least from the interest, of many readers. And the very nature of such diction, the sheer length and complexity of some of the words, would require proportionally long sentences:

> Psephologists contend that the volatility of the electorate is a consequence of the socio-economic re-alignment of British

society and society's disillusionment with traditional ideological politics, but the geographic polarisation of Britain into regions of deprivation surrounding an area of metropolitan affluence could bring about a revival of partisan voting patterns.

This prose style might be acceptable in a leader article or a political feature in one of the broadsheet Sunday newspapers or in a political weekly, but it is not acceptable as news writing and it would not normally be acceptable in a local newspaper; the diction produces such a thick texture, and the sentence structure such a convoluted pattern, that the reader has difficulty in understanding the meaning. Even the most intelligent reader would have some difficulty in making complete sense of so many ideas and assumptions on a single reading of the sentence.

The prose style would then be wrong because it would be drawing attention to itself rather than directing the readers' attention to the meaning the writer is trying to convey. Other examples of combinations of diction and sentence structure appear at the end of this section.

The ideal diction is not any single one of those outlined above but a choice of words that is most appropriate for the subject of the newspaper story and for the newspaper's readers.

Sentence structure and paragraph structure

But diction is only one element of prose style. The other main elements are sentence and paragraph structures, punctuation schemes, rhythm and tone.

The short sentence can be effective. It can be one of the main elements in a taut prose style. This style can convey meaning forcefully and economically. If it does this it will be acceptable to the reader. But repeated short sentences can set up abrupt, staccato rhythms. The style then becomes mannered. It may become selfconsciously terse, as this paragraph shows. And when the mannerism becomes obvious to the readers then they may be distracted by the mechanics of the prose style rather than informed by the underlying meaning.

The short sentence can convey a sense of tension or drama and it is therefore essential in most news stories, but even there the short sentences should sometimes give way to a longer sentence if the story is to hold the readers' attention.

And in longer news stories and in feature articles the exclusive use of short sentences could be too limited, too inflexible to capture the full detail, the subtlety or complexity, of the real story.

Longer sentences allow the writer to create variations in the rhythm of his prose style, and at the same time they introduce suppleness, fluency and resonance. But longer sentences must be used sparingly and must be firmly controlled, especially when they contain large numbers of polysyllabic words, lest these sentence structures seduce the journalist into constructing elaborate patterns in which the meaning, and the readers, are lost.

Another essential reason for control is that the physical restriction of column width in newspapers and magazines means that too many long sentences, or even one extended sentence, will show up as an unrelieved and unappealing lump of copy on the page.

Paragraph structure should be determined by the kind of sentence structures the writer is using, by the content of the story he is writing, and by concern for the reader.

If the average sentence is fairly short, as it should be in most news writing, then the paragraphs should be proportionally short. Here again the physical limit of column width should be a useful reminder about length; too many unbroken column inches can look ugly and intimidating to the readers.

Paragraphing is also determined by the content of the story. A new paragraph should normally be opened to introduce separate aspects of a story, so that the paragraph structure reflects the story's structure, a new paragraph indicating a new development — a different person, a quotation, an event or incident — in the story.

Punctuation schemes

Punctuation is essentially an aid to the meaning of a piece of writing. For example, the two sentences:

He says he will re-write the story.

and

He says: 'He will re-write the story!'

use exactly the same diction and syntax, that is, the same

words in the same word order, but the first sentence refers to one person only — the person who agrees to re-write his own story — while the second sentence refers to two persons, one of whom speaks emphatically about another. It is the difference in punctuation that reveals the difference in meaning between these two sentences. (The punctuation of direct speech will be examined in detail later.)

The meaning of a statement can be changed by the simplest of punctuation marks:

A last, minute effort brought a goal for the home team.
or, more probably
A last-minute effort brought a goal for the home team.

The simple difference between a comma and a hyphen changes the meaning of these sentences in which diction and syntax are identical. It is simple punctuation again that illustrates the difference between: 'The reporter bought a little, used car' and 'The reporter bought a little-used car', between 'He interviewed the City's old-time 'keeper' and 'He interviewed the city's old time-keeper', and between 'the high street' and 'the High Street'. The do-it-yourself instruction that stated 'remove tie on cover' instead of 'remove tie-on cover' caused some frustration. One of the most comprehensive guides to punctuation is *Mind the Stop* by G V Carey (Pelican Books), and there is a helpful chapter on punctuation in *A Journalist's Guide To The Use Of English* by Ted Bottomley and Anthony Loftus (Star Publications, Wolverhampton).

Prose rhythm

Punctuation is more than an aid to meaning. A punctuation scheme will have a marked effect on the rhythm of your prose, and it is generally the case that a lightly punctuated passage of prose will flow more smoothly than a heavily punctuated passage. On the general question of punctuation it is sometimes helpful to compare the written word with the spoken word: a densely punctuated passage of prose is comparable to a speech that is marked by pauses of varying length, changes in vocal inflection, and changes of tempo; a lightly punctuated passage of prose is comparable to fluent, continuous speech.

The fluency of rhythm that comes from a lighter punctuation

scheme is always preferable to the hesitancy or the ponderous rhetoric that is sometimes the result of a heavy punctuation scheme. Examples of differently weighted punctuation schemes applied to different forms of diction appear at the end of this section.

Tone

Every time you speak, your words are uttered in a noticeable tone of voice. The tone is produced not only by the words and sentences you speak but also by a combination of physiological factors like vocal cords, by your attitude or intention in the act of speaking, and by the intensity, that is, the pace and volume, of your speech.

Tone in a passage of writing is roughly comparable to tone of voice, with the obvious difference that your written tone is the result of your particular use of the various written elements that make up your prose style, especially your diction. This chapter has already shown that your choice of diction — concrete or abstract, monosyllabic or polysyllabic, neutral or emotive — can have a marked effect on the tone of a piece of writing.

In a newspaper some of the most obvious examples of the deliberate use of tone appear in the advertisements. Holiday advertisements invite you to 'bask in golden sunlight' rather than experience an average daily temperature of 25°C, and to 'wine and dine until midnight beneath the velvet skies' rather than eat and drink until 24.00 hours in the open air. Property advertisers speak of houses being in 'superb decorative order' when they mean the house does not need to be painted and decorated immediately. And if the house is described as 'ideal for conversion' it is probably dilapidated.

But tone can also be apparent in news writing. For example, a passage written in formal, polysyllabic diction with upper case spellings and contained in long, heavily punctuated sentences would have a tone that would almost certainly be serious, could possibly be solemn or sombre, and might even seem pompous:

Mr Wilfred Nugent MP, in a letter to his Constituency Party, has intimated his decision — which he reached after careful consideration of all relevant factors, as well as prolonged soul-searching — to decline to accept nomination as the Parliamentary Candidate at the next General Election.

In contrast to this, a passage that uses some emotive diction in short, lightly punctuated sentences could create a tone that seems aggressive or even sensational:

> Furious Wallfield residents slammed the local council yesterday. A deluge of complaints jammed the council switchboard. Callers claimed the roads department was guilty of criminal negligence. The department had made no attempt at snow-clearing or road-gritting, residents said.

Economy of language

This chapter and the chapter on the news story have shown that one of the most distinctive features of good prose style in news writing is economy of language. Aspects of this economy are diction that has a greater number of concrete, monosyllabic words than abstract, polysyllabic words; sentences and paragraphs that are varied but firmly controlled in their length and structure; light rather than dense punctuation; and a level, dispassionate tone.

Pressure of space in a newspaper along with the restriction of column width will force the writer to practise economy of language, but there are other more positive reasons for adopting an economic style. An obvious reason is that the aim of the news story is to go straight to the point of any set of circumstances, reporting the main facts with a sense of immediacy and omitting all irrelevant material. The very nature of the news story demands economy of language.

In contrast, the language of legal documents, the 'officialese' of some national and local government communications, and the highly specialised language of academic or scientific papers show that the meaning of a piece of writing is sometimes obscured rather than revealed by the writer's use of language:

> The planning officer intimated that there were adequate toilet facilities in the immediate area at this moment in time but he expressed a favourable attitude towards conducting a survey in order to assess the requirements for the future.

Some writers are obscure because they can write in no other way, and their lack of clarity of expression is the result of a lack of clarity of thought. Some writers — particularly in the academic world — practise a deliberate obscurity in an attempt to impress their colleagues and rivals; the result can be a linguistic contortion that invites ridicule.

The prose style of the good journalist has a deceptive simplicity. The simplicity is not 'natural' but is in fact achieved through the constant, self-critical practice of the craft of writing. It is not 'easier' than the more ornate or rhetorical styles, some of which can be highly self-indulgent, but is in fact more difficult since it demands rigorous professional discipline. Above all else, the prose style of the good journalist combines two paramount concerns: factual accuracy and courtesy to the reader.

An ideal prose style?

The ideal prose style, like the ideal diction, is not any single set of elements but the combination of those elements that are most appropriate to the subject of the story and to the reader.

In feature articles and in longer works of fiction or travel or biography the writer can develop a style that is recognisably his own until his personal prose style becomes a literary persona, an aspect of his identity that he discovers and cultivates through the act of writing and through the printed word. But there is no place for a journalist's personality in news writing.

In news writing the most effective prose style is one that is imperceptible to most of the readers. It is a style that brings together the main elements of prose composition — diction, sentence and paragraph structure, punctuation, rhythm and tone — in a strictly relevant and seemingly effortless way so that the meaning of the news story seems to pass simply and spontaneously from the printed page to the mind of the reader.

Together, these qualities of strict relevance, effortlessness, simplicity and spontaneity are the seal of professionalism in news writing. The qualities are not natural gifts. They are aspects of a craft that have to be achieved through constant practice and a lasting interest in life and in language. Even if these qualities are achieved they will not be fixed and permanent features of a writer's prose style but ideals that have to be rediscovered and re-affirmed with every assignment. The complete professional is the writer who feels that his professionalism is never quite complete.

Prose style exercises

Analyse the prose style of the following passages, commenting on the diction, sentence and paragraph structures, punctuation, prose rhythm, and tone.

Explain why these passages would not be acceptable as news writing, and re-write the passages in a style that would be acceptable.

1 Councillor Harry Dean, who has been active in local politics for over thirty years, during which time he has held the office of Mayor of Glasborough, is presently Chairman of the Leisure and Recreation Committee of Glasborough District Council, in which position he is the elected Councillor responsible for the disbursement of a substantial budget (in excess of one and three-quarter million pounds per annum) for the provision of an extensive range of cultural, social and sporting facilities and amenities.

2 Readers may be interested to learn, if they did not already know, that the art of coarse debating is alive and well in Wallfield District Council. On Wednesday last a full meeting of the District Council debated the proposal that dogs should be banned from the Wallside Memorial Park. In a prolonged and somewhat heated debate (one councillor offered to engage in fisticuffs with his opponents) dogs were accused of everything from vandalising municipal flower beds to devouring children and spreading the black death. Seldom have I heard so much doggerel under one woof.

3 All members of the work force of Wallside Engineering Supplies Ltd, a total of 375 employees, have been made compulsorily redundant because of the closure of the company, a major source of employment in the town, following the acquisition of Wallside Engineering by Metropolitan Assets plc. The closure has affected not only the 375 persons immediately involved but has had the additional consequence

81

of depressing employment in the ancillary industries which supplied Wallside Engineering, and is having a further detrimental effect on local retail trades, evidence of which can be seen in the vacant premises in Wallfield High Street.

4   Forensic scientists will carefully examine the blackened remains of Glasborough's renowned Stag's Head Hotel which was tragically destroyed by a savage fire last night despite the valiant efforts of the gallant Glasborough Fire Brigade, ably assisted by the conscientious officers of Glasborough Police Force.

5   Furious Wallfield businessmen lashed out at the District Council last week.

Mr Victor Wilson, the highly respected president of Wallfield Chamber of Commerce, slammed Kevin Armitage, controversial chairman of the council's finance committee.

The traders were hitting out at the shock 18% rates rise. The rates bombshell was announced last week.

Mr Armitage said the rise would save local services for the poor and needy. But he would say that, wouldn't he?

Mr Wilson said costs would spiral and force traders to cut back on staff. Unemployment would soar because of the rates rise.

Local traders, said Mr Armitage snidely, were only interested in profits, not people.

Exercises in economy of language

Re-write the following sentences in a more economic prose style:

1   The Glasborough batsman sustained an injury to his left wrist and was taken to hospital for x-ray purposes.

2   No one was allowed anywhere near the vicinity of the building due to the fact that there was an ongoing demolition operation in process.

3   The company submitted an application for planning permission for a hotel with 50 units of bedroom accommodation and with ample provision for car-parking facilities.

4 Inadequate provision was made for shopping facilities due to the fact that members of the public were not involved in the consultation process.

5 The Member of Parliament for Walls and Dalesmoor North has stated his willingness to give active consideration to the petition bearing the signatures of the greater proportion of the population of North Dale.

6 Tenants in the flats above Dempster's Disco in Albert Street, Wallfield have lodged complaints about the noise, which they say is of an excessive level.

7 Wallfield magistrates refused to extend a lenient attitude towards the accused by the name of Anthony Fielding who had been convicted time and time again.

8 Teachers in two Wallfield schools walked out in protest at the exact same time and brought about a cessation of teaching operations.

9 He alerted the chairman to the fact that the hall might be filled to its maximum capacity because a greater number of parents intended to be in attendance at the meeting.

10 The Wallfield defender committed a foul on the Glasborough forward, and consequent to this incident there was an outbreak of fighting among the supporters of the rival teams.

11 Glasborough police succeeded in putting an end to the fight but three officers suffered injuries of a minor nature.

12 The accused tendered a plea of guilty to the charge of breach of the peace, but he pointed out that this was the first time he had committed the offence.

13 The finance committee of Glasborough District Council met for the purpose of deciding the annual budget for the year but the decision was postponed until a later date.

14 Councillor Braithwaite, who had not previously put in an appearance at the finance committee, attended in his capacity as chairman of the transport group for which he proceeded to demand additional financial resources.

15 The South Dale planning officer intimated that there were adequate toilet facilities in the vicinity at this moment in time but he expressed a favourable attitude towards conducting a survey in order to assess the requirements for the future.

16 The photographer failed to arrive on time due to the fact that his car was delayed by adverse weather conditions.

17 The editor of the Wallfield Mercury is of the opinion that the local correspondent for South Dale is someone who cannot be relied upon since the correspondent does not use language in an economic way.

18 Human error is the main contributory factor in the majority of instances of industrial accidents.

19 A machine operator was dismissed from employment at Glasborough Timber Services after being warned three times in writing about being absent from work without good reason.

20 Thieves who committed a robbery at a Glasborough antique shop from which they stole antiques worth over £15,000 made good their escape by heading in a southerly direction.

Exercises in punctuation

Punctuate the following statements:

1 whats the line youre taking in next weeks feature on womens rights

2 the special branch removed files notebooks video tapes transcripts correspondence and press cuttings from the bbcs glasgow office

3 whose copy of whos who is this if its still got its dust jacket its yours isnt it

4 newspapers and newspaper proprietors have changed since the 1950s and 60s many 50s newspapers for example had only advertisements on the front page news was on the inside pages

5 as he stepped off the flying scotsman the scotsman tripped and sent the scotsman flying

6   the editor asked the leader writer to check the times today and today tomorrow and to watch this weeks this week next week

7   he put the mail on sunday on the sunday express and the sunday express in the mail on sunday

8   wheres your story theirs are there but theres no sign of yours

9   the telegraphs air correspondent watched the take off fly past and some minutes later the safe touch down of planes which in the words of the mod news release were described only as newly designed top secret swing winged military aircraft

10   were just as short staffed as we were last week if the chief reporters still ill ill sub the paper myself hell hell have to get well well all be ill if he doesnt

7

NEWS SUMMARY

Summary is an essential discipline for reporters. It can also be a demanding discipline, one which requires that the journalist be able to identify the most important or the most interesting facts in a lengthy document — a document that may be written in a highly specialised or highly turgid language — and present those facts in an accurate, readable news story or news paragraph.

News summary

The annual report of a local company or of a university in the circulation area of a local newspaper, the findings of a local planning enquiry, the manifesto of a political party in the local constituency, booklets from the regional tourist authority, a policy statement from the chamber of commerce — these publications could be of interest to a local newspaper. But since the publications may run to several thousand words they could not possibly be published in full in the local press. At a national level, the report of a Royal Commission or Parliamentary select committee or a major public enquiry may be of national interest but if the reports run to hundreds of pages and many thousands of words then no newspaper can present the reports in their entirety.

Even if a newspaper were willing to allocate several pages to a major report, it is unlikely that the average reader could spare the time to read it. But if the report contains material of interest to the reader then it must be summarised for publication.

Since the summary will normally take the form of a news story, the journalist should regard the reading of the raw material as a news-gathering exercise. He should select only those facts that have news value and reject all other material.

The summary as news story, in contrast to the academic or business summary, will seldom follow the sequence of information as it appears in the original document. The news summary normally requires radical restructuring as well as a drastic reduction in the length of the original material.

Another difference between the news summary and some academic summaries is that the news summary will use the language of the original unless the source material has to be paraphrased to make it intelligible to the reader, or has to be recast from direct speech to reported speech. If it proves necessary to change the wording of the original document this should be done without changing the original meaning.

The words may be different but the meaning must be the same. And the end result must be an accurate, cohesive, interesting news story.

Techniques of summary

The journalist can use several techniques to achieve this result, and the first of these techniques is the approach to the source material. It is pointless to suggest, as academic textbooks do, that the source material be read systematically twice over from start to finish. This is a useless recommendation when the original documents run to hundreds of pages. And the acute pressure of time, especially on the daily newspaper, or the limited number of reporters on the local newspaper, means that the journalist must be highly selective.

Use the contents page as a guide to the most important or interesting sections of the original publication. If there is no contents page or no index, you can often save time by beginning at the end of the source material.

In the majority of reports — Parliamentary select committees, Royal Commissions, public enquiries, annual reports and others — the information of greatest interest to the journalist is most likely to be found in those sections of the report headed 'Findings' or 'Conclusions and Recommendations', or 'The Future', or 'The Way Ahead'. These sections usually appear in the closing chapters or closing pages of reports, and it is there that you are most likely to find your news story and your intro.

Begin at the end, and as you read the findings or the

recommendations or the statement on the way ahead remember that the importance of the original material is the extent to which its contents will affect the lives or catch the interest of the readers of your newspaper. The original material is unlikely to include a specific reference to the villages or to the town or city in your circulation area; it is your responsibility to see what impact the report may have on your readers.

If the language of the source material is intelligible to the general reader you should include direct quotations — key phrases, sentences, or even short paragraphs — in your news summary. If the language of the source is too highly specialised — the language of science, medicine, or government 'officialese' — then the news summary will be written mainly in reported speech with only a few words or phrases quoted directly from the source.

The inclusion of quotations is desirable because this can give a similar effect to that of a news story which uses quotes from an interview. The use of quotations confirms the authenticity of the news story, gives an immediacy to the facts and is sometimes a graphic illustration of these facts, and the interaction of quotes and reported speech brings an added energy to a news story. As a rough guide, to which there will of course be exceptions, the most effective mix of reported speech and quotes in the news summary is likely to be two thirds reported speech and one third quotes.

But even when a news summary has this mix, is accurate and cohesive, observes economy of language, is well structured with a good intro and strong narrative flow, even then the news summary will not be acceptable as a news story unless it is immediately intelligible to the average reader. The report on which the news summary is based may be the end result of a long enquiry into an event or a set of circumstances — a fatal accident in your town, a planning proposal or planning objection, the training or staffing needs of a national industry which has a branch in your circulation area — the origin of which may have been forgotten by the average reader. In such cases the journalist should remind the reader of the story's origin and significance, and this can be done subtly and unobtrusively in an early paragraph, perhaps paragraph three, of the news summary. The information needed for the explanation may be in the introduction to the report, or it may exist in a more manageable form in the newspaper's cuttings library.

Similarly, if the subject of the original report is important but abstruse — the chemical content of food additives, or the effect of the exchange rate on the export performance of a local industry — then the reporter should consult someone with expert knowledge of the subject and get an authoritative, attributable quote which the readers will understand. Alternatively, the reporter should explain the subject in simple terms at an early stage in the story.

In this respect, the inclusion of explanatory or even extraneous material, the news summary is again different from the academic summary. A further difference is that the news summary should use examples and brief case studies, comparisons and catalogues that may appear in the original if this material helps to give the story more colour, more credibility, and above all more humanity in the eyes of the reader.

Summary summarised

The techniques of summary can themselves be summarised.

1 Treat the assignment as a news-gathering exercise, and write your news summary as a news story.

2 Use the contents page or the index of the source material to identify the most important or most interesting information.

3 Where there is no contents page or index look first at the later chapters or pages of a report, especially those sections entitled 'Findings', 'Conclusions', 'Recommendations', or 'The Way Ahead'.

4 Open your news summary with a good news intro.

5 Stay close to the wording of the original material unless it is too specialised or too turgid for your reader, in which case paraphrase the original without changing the meaning.

6 Use a mix of reported speech and quotations.

7 Insert explanatory material — a phrase, a sentence, or even a short paragraph — if this is needed to remind your readers of the origin of the story.

8 Include an intelligible quotation from an authoritative source if this will help to clarify the meaning of the story.

9 Include examples and comparisons which appear in the original if these help to strengthen the story.

10 Check that the end result is in fact a news story — factual, self-explanatory, and interesting.

Exercises in news summary

Here is an example of how an original passage can be rewritten as a news summary. Firstly, the original passage:

BLOOD SPORTS — POPULAR OR ELITIST CULTURE?

In the nineteenth century as in the twentieth sports involving animals were among the great popular cultures. Bear-baiting, bull-baiting, badger-baiting, cock-fighting, dog-fighting, and cock-throwing were all popular sports in the nineteenth century. (Cock-throwing involved tying a cockerel to a stake and then throwing stones at it.) All these sports were outlawed in the nineteenth century after hundreds of years of existence, and it would seem that the legislation has been a form of education since most British people now regard these blood sports with revulsion.

But other sports which involved the killing of animals were not outlawed. Stag-hunting, fox-hunting, otter-hunting, and hare-coursing all survived into the present century and some still survive today, as does deer-stalking and the shooting of game birds. The question arises: why were some of these sports outlawed while others remain?

It is sometimes argued that the essential difference is that in one type of blood sport, baiting, the animal was almost always killed or mutilated for the pleasure of the spectators who did not themselves confront the animal, whereas in the other type of sport, hunting, the animal had a chance of survival and the sportsman was — so some would argue — an equal participant in the chase.

But another important difference was the social and economic division between the two classes of spectator. Animal baiting and fighting were popular sports in the sense that they were supported by the common people; animal hunting, especially on horseback, was supported by a much smaller social group, the group which included those persons who made and enforced the law.

The law-makers and the law-enforcers banned those blood sports which appealed to the peasants and common citizens but retained other sports in which they, the middle and upper classes, indulged.

News summary of BLOOD SPORTS — POPULAR OR ELITIST CULTURE?

A step-by-step method of summarising the passage is as follows:

Open the news summary with the essential information in the final sentence. This sentence, which is itself a summary of the passage, can be treated as an intro if we include the words, 'nineteenth century', to let the reader know the historical period.

> Nineteenth century law-makers banned blood sports which appealed to the common people but kept sports in which they, the middle and upper classes, indulged. That is the conclusion of an article, 'Blood Sports — Popular or Elitist Culture?', published this week.

Continue the summary with illustrative information from paragraphs 1 and 2 of the original, but be selective:

> Bear-baiting and cock-fighting, were outlawed but the hunting of stags, foxes, and otters survived.

Continue with the argument from paragraph 3:

> Some argue that baiting killed or mutilated the animal to please spectators who were not at risk, whereas the huntsman was an equal participant and the animal might survive.

End with essential information from paragraph 4 of the original:

> But social class was another important difference. Baiting was for the common people while hunting was supported by a small minority which included the makers and enforcers of law.

The final news summary then reads:

Patrick Napier   7 June   Baiting — 1

Nineteenth century law-makers banned blood sports which appealed to the common people but kept sports in which they, the middle and upper classes, indulged. That is the conclusion of an article, 'Blood Sports — Popular or Elitist Culture?', published this week.

Bear-baiting and cock-fighting were outlawed but the hunting of stags, foxes and otters survived.

Some argue that baiting killed or mutilated the animal to please spectators who were not at risk, whereas the huntsman was an equal participant and the animal might survive.

But social class was another important difference. Baiting was for the common people while hunting was supported by a small minority which included the makers and enforcers of law.

End

Some important points have had to be omitted. These include legislation as a form of education, and public revulsion in para 1, the question in para 2, and the word 'horseback' in para 4. Even so, this 115-word summary retains the language and the meaning of the original.

Exercises

Write a news summary of this passage in not more than 120 words.

COMMUNICATION IN ORGANISATIONS

Communication in large formal organisations — industrial, commercial, educational — should be humane as well as efficient because communication is the essential element in human relations. If the quality of communication in the organisation is completely impersonal and ignores the humanity of its members, then these members may develop attitudes of indifference, anxiety or hostility towards the organisation. The attitudes may find expression in patterns of behaviour which reduce the efficiency of the organisation: negligence, absenteeism, disruptive behaviour, or resignations. If the quality of communication, and with it the quality of human relations, is particularly bad then some people in the organisation may develop psychosomatic symptoms; that is, forms of distress which are psychological in origin but which manifest themselves in physical ways such as stomach pains, headaches, backaches, and giddiness. Although it may be difficult to establish precise cases of cause and effect, there are strong connections between the quality of communication in an organisation and the wellbeing of that organisation's members.

The chief executive and management of an organisation are sometimes tempted to operate a policy of 'minimum communication', but this too might be seen as impersonal and could bring about the conditions outlined above. A policy of minimum communication could have other unfortunate results. The ordinary members of the organisation might feel that the management was being secretive, in which case hostility between management and members would intensify. And when there is little or no communication in a human situation then people inevitably fill the information vacuum with 'information' of their own: rumour, gossip, speculation, fantasy, and cynicism. This is a normal response to a lack of communication, and it is better that the vacuum be filled with relevant, reasonable and humane communication. The ordinary members of the organisation will then have a sense of purpose in what they do; they may also have a sense of community amongst themselves and even with the management of the organisation.

Write a news summary of the following passage in not more than 150 words.

INGROWN NEWS VALUES

News values are not always the same as human values, but if reporters and news editors allow too wide a gap to grow between the two, or if reporters and editors become preoccupied by news values to the exclusion of all other values, then there is a risk that news values will become ingrown.

The risk is greater for large daily newspapers than it is for local newspapers. The local paper has a smaller and more precisely defined readership, the editorial staff usually live within the paper's circulation area as members of the local community, and the editor is often an active member of that community, all of which should mean that the local newspaper is more attentive to the values of the society in which it exists. If a newspaper ignores those values and concentrates exclusively on what it sees as 'newsman's' news, then distortions begin to creep in.

A common distortion is to highlight conflict and controversy while disregarding areas of agreement, and when the element of conflict is exaggerated it follows almost inevitably that personalities will be emphasised at the expense of policies and issues. Similarly, a newspaper may give greater prominence to stories which contain accounts of physical action than to more important stories that contain ideas.

Newspapers rightly keep a watch on their competitors but they sometimes watch each other so intently that they end up writing the same or similar stories. News values will always have a tendency to become ingrown if editors do their news-gathering from each other's pages.

But a newspaper can also become trapped by its own particular obsessions. What may have begun as a genuine and highly commendable campaign against illicit drugs or football hooliganism or child abuse may become a wilful determination to find examples of these things where none exist.

Yet another distortion, much more obvious in the national daily and Sunday press than in local weeklies, is the stereotyping — and thus the misrepresentation — of individuals and groups. Stereotyping can all too easily turn ugly. Political, religious or ethnic minorities, social deviants or dissidents who are entirely innocent of any offence, may be exposed to public ridicule or even hatred.

These distortions which arise from ingrown news values are comparatively rare in the local press because the local newspaper constantly matches its news values against the wider values of the society it exists to serve. If it ignores those wider values the newspaper may in turn be ignored by the people who hold the values — the readers.

Write a news summary of this passage in not more than 120 words.

THE ADVERTISING DEBATE

The contested issues in the advertising industry are partly moral and partly economic. The case against advertising could be put in these terms.

Mass consumer advertising, by appealing to our appetites and acquisitiveness, is stimulating some of the baser human impulses such as greed, vanity, and self-indulgence, and may be doing so at the expense of more admirable impulses. And some consumer advertising for products such as soaps, cosmetics, and household detergents deliberately attempts to foster a sense of inadequacy in women as persons or as wives and mothers.

It can also be argued that it is irresponsible to emphasise consumption when we live in a world of limited resources which are unevenly divided amongst the world's population and which in some cases, for example oil and other minerals, should be carefully conserved rather than rapidly consumed. By promoting this getting and spending, this acquisition and consumption of goods and services, the advertiser may be influencing not only our spending habits but our wider view of life, since the advertiser encourages us to see all things as commodities which are available at a price.

The economic counter-argument to this is that since mass consumer advertising promotes mass marketing in a mass society, the abolition of such advertising would have disastrous results. If advertising were to cease then consumption might fall; if consumption were to fall then production would have to be reduced; and if production were reduced then employment would have to fall proportionally. The resulting unemployment would be a greater social evil than the alleged social evil of advertising.

But a more direct economic argument is that most British news media depend on advertising for their survival. All in-dependent radio and television companies receive the bulk of their income — over 95% — from advertising revenue, and some newspapers and magazines receive over 70% of their income from advertising. Without this income from advertising these media would cease to exist.

8

QUOTE... UNQUOTE — DIRECT SPEECH

In court cases, in local council meetings, at news conferences, in Parliament and in interviews the news is to be found in the statements people make. The accurate use of direct speech — colloquially known as a quote or quotes — is essential when a news story is based entirely or largely on the spoken word.

Direct Speech

In other news stories the use of quotations, as we have already seen, can make the story more credible and more interesting. A statement from a person centrally involved in an event can bring a genuine element of human drama — or 'human interest' — to the story. The actual words of an eye-witness can bring graphic immediacy to a report of an accident, a fire or a crime. A quote from a policeman or fireman can confirm the authenticity of the story and can also give important information on the initial cause or the final outcome of an incident. A quote from an authoritative source — and preferably an independent source such as a scientist at a local university or college — can sometimes clarify the story and explain its fuller significance. The skilful use of quotes can inject a legitimate energy into a story, and the interaction of quotes and reported speech can generate a creative tension in the news story.

The importance of direct speech, or quotes, in a news story is clear. The journalist must also be confident about the techniques and mechanics of using quotes.

Techniques of direct speech

Identify the speaker

Always identify the person who is being quoted for the first time before you quote his or her words.

Do not write:

> 'The procession was diverted to avoid the possibility of confrontation between the marchers and the crowds arriving for the replay of the Wallfield-Glasborough cup-tie on Wednesday night,' said Chief Inspector George Bell of Walls and Dalesmoor Police.

The reader does not discover the identity of the speaker, and thus the reason for the quotation, until the end of the sentence. Do not make the reader wait; instead, identify the speaker before you quote him:

> Chief Inspector George Bell of Walls and Dalesmoor Police said: 'The procession was diverted to avoid the possibility of confrontation between the marchers and the crowds arriving for the replay of the Wallfield-Glasborough cup-tie on Wednesday night.'

By first identifying the speaker in this way you make clear to the reader the relevance and significance of the quote that follows. If in the same story you use further quotes from Chief Inspector George Bell of Walls and Dalesmoor Police, then the speaker should be referred to as Chief Inspector Bell. And when his identity is clearly established Chief Inspector Bell can of course be referred to simply as 'he'.

Punctuation

The words actually spoken must be contained within inverted commas. Inverted commas, or quotation marks, are also known colloquially as quotes. The fact that the same word, 'quotes', is used for the punctuation marks and for the direct speech contained within those marks is a possible source of confusion. You can avoid ambiguity by referring to the punctuation as inverted commas or quotation marks, and the words spoken as quotations or direct speech.

The choice of double or single inverted commas — " " or ' '

— will be decided for you by the house style of your newspaper. Examples here will normally use single inverted commas.

The final punctuation mark at the end of the quotation — a full stop, a question mark, or an exclamation mark — should be inside the inverted commas when the quotation is the main part of a full sentence:

> A spokesman for Wallfield Royal Infirmary said: 'A five-year-old boy was admitted with minor burns to his hands and arms last night.'

The full stop is inside the closing inverted commas. But if the direct speech is contained within reported speech as part of a longer sentence, then the full stop should be at the end of the complete sentence:

> What the reporter said was: 'I'll cover the Deanvale Community Council meeting tonight' as he left the office.

The convention is that there must be only one full stop and that it must appear at the end of the complete sentence. The quotation above cannot be punctuated with a full stop because the quotation is not the end of the sentence.

But the convention is not entirely logical because the other end-punctuation marks — the question mark and the exclamation mark — can appear inside the closing inverted commas when the quotation is contained within reported speech:

> What the reporter said was: 'Will I cover the Deanvale Community Council meeting tonight?' as he left the office.

The question mark refers only to the quotation and not to the longer statement. Similarly, in the sentence:

> As the reporter left the office the editor shouted: 'Cover the meeting of the Deanvale Community Council tonight!'

the exclamation mark refers only to the quotation.

A sentence cannot normally take more than one full stop but it can take more than one question mark:

> Why do you think he asked: 'Is the Wallfield Mercury's circulation holding up?' when he met you yesterday?

Two question marks are needed because two questions are being asked, one by the words in direct speech and the other by the statement that surrounds the direct speech. Two question marks are also needed when we have a quotation inside a longer quotation:

> 'Why do you think he asked: "Is the Wallfield Mercury's circulation holding up?" when he met you yesterday?' the editor asked.

But note what happens to the question marks when the end of the internal quotation coincides with the end of the sentence which is itself in direct speech:

> The editor said: 'When he met you yesterday why do you think he asked: "Is the Wallfield Mercury's circulation holding up?" '

The logic of the sentence requires two question marks but the effect at the end of the sentence would be too absurdly cluttered:

> ' "Is the Wallfield Mercury's circulation holding up?"?'

The logically correct punctuation would in fact look wrong, as would two full stops punctuating a quotation inside a quotation at the end of a sentence: .".' The full stop should be between the double and single inverted commas at the end of the complete statement:

> The editor added: 'That quote from the manager should read: "The first goal was offside".'

The examples quoted above illustrate other conventions in the punctuation of direct speech. When a passage in direct speech includes a statement from another speaker or another source — that is, when you have a quote within a quote — use a simple scheme of double and single inverted commas to distinguish one from the other:

> She said: 'I liked your story — "Glasborough girl wins national art award" — in the Gazette last week.'

Paragraphs

When the actual words of one speaker extend over two or more paragraphs, the inverted commas are re-opened at the start of each new paragraph but they are not closed until the end of the quotation:

A spokeswoman for Wallfield Royal Infirmary said: 'A five-year-old boy was admitted with minor burns to his hands and arms last night.

'The boy has been examined by our burns unit consultant, who confirmed that there are no complications. The patient is in a comfortable condition and he will be released tomorrow.

'I should prefer not to comment on whether the police have interviewed the boy about the cause of the fire.'

When a new speaker or a different speaker is quoted you must of course open a new paragraph:

The leader of the majority Conservative group said: 'I take this opportunity to welcome the newly elected members of Glasborough District Council, and I hope all members will work together for the good of the people of Glasborough.'

'Thank you for your welcome,' said the new Alliance member. 'I will certainly support reasonable, moderate and liberal policies.'

'Then you've come to the wrong place, mate,' said the Labour group leader.

The reporting verb

The examples above illustrate the punctuation of the reporting verb. When the reporting verb appears before the words actually quoted — and this will always be the case when you are introducing a speaker for the first time — the newspaper convention is that the verb is punctuated by a colon:

The editor said: 'I want you to cover the meeting of the finance committee.'

When the reporting verb appears after the quotation, the punctuation mark — normally a comma, a question mark or an exclamation mark — will be determined by the nature of the quotation:

'I want you to cover the meeting of the finance committee,' the editor said.

or

'How would you like to cover the meeting of the finance committee?' the editor asked.

or

'Cover the meeting of the finance committee!' the editor ordered.

Sometimes the reporting verb will be contained within the quotation. This simple technique maintains the continuity of the quotation and at the same time allows you to vary your sentence structure and re-affirm the identity of the speaker:

'And when you've covered the finance committee,' the editor added, 'I want you to telephone the infirmary to see how that five-year-old boy is progressing.'

The reporting verb should be as simple as the quotation allows. Do not use reporting verbs like 'mused', 'opined', 'expostulated', 'interjected' or 'remonstrated'. Your readers may not readily understand these words, and such self-consciously clever diction distracts the readers' attention from the quotation and from the story.

Use reporting verbs like 'said', 'stated', and 'asked'. If a quotation is extended do not write: 'he went on to say' or 'he continued by saying'; instead, simply write: 'he added' or 'he continued'. Other reporting verbs such as 'explained', 'insisted', 'repeated' or 'denied' should be used only when they are needed to clarify the nature of the quotation.

Titles

A final example of newspaper practice is worth noting. When a newspaper quotes from a written source — a company's annual report, a local council planning document, a leaflet or manifesto from a political party, a recently published book — then the actual words quoted will be clearly contained within inverted commas. But it is current practice in some newspapers not to punctuate the title of the report or the book.

The convention in academic circles is to underline the title: Local Government in Britain, and the convention in book publishing is to print the title in italics: *Local Government in Britain*. Other options are to punctuate the title with inverted commas: 'Local Government in Britain', or to print the title in upper case characters: LOCAL GOVERNMENT IN BRITAIN.

Some newspapers use none of these devices, and the result can sometimes be confusing or even unintentionally amusing:

Local Government in Britain was reviewed by the specialist journals.

Tonight producers broke new ground in television.

Tess is remarkably faithful to Hardy's original.

The Kentish Express arrived on time.

Admiral Alexeyevitch limped into harbour.

The confusion could or course be eliminated by using any of the typesetting devices discussed above, but repeated practice has established the convention of unpunctuated titles, and convention is a powerful force in newspapers and elsewhere.

Exercises in punctuation — direct speech

Punctuate the following:

1 why did you lead with labour fury at rent vote the reporter asked

2 mrs irene catto winner of this weeks evening echo spot the ball contest said ive already booked a round the world cruise on the canberra

3 i liked your review of the concert by smoking armpits said sheila from the mercurys tele ads department really said danny the new reporter have you heard their new album schitzophrenia

4 a spokeswoman for glasboroughs mayfield theatre said well stage more popular productions this year for example shaws arms and the man and cowards blithe spirit in an attempt to recoup last years loss

5 were you surprised by the disciplinary committees decision the reporter asked wallfield united chairman harold hampson said a month long five game suspension is a shocker isnt it do you feel shermans punishment is justified well to be honest we expected something drastic this time said the chairman but i want to go on record as saying sammys a victim of his reputation more than anything what do you mean asked the reporter i mean hes been a marked man ever since he broke that linesmans leg last year remember sammy went to tackle

the glasborough striker missed him and bumped into the linesman broke his leg didnt he dont you think said the reporter people make a habit of breaking things when shermans playing legs collar bones ribs that sort of thing sammys a big strong boy said the chairman sammys got commitment commitment and a one month suspension said the reporter

9

REPORTED SPEECH

News is frequently to be found in the spoken word, as the previous chapter, 'Quote . . . Unquote', shows, but a problem for the reporter is that on many occasions the speakers will say too much. This chapter shows how the reporter can restructure a speech in the form of an accurate news story.

Reported speech

You have some control over the length and content of an interview, and when you have gathered enough information you can bring the interview to an end. But you will find that you have no control over local councillors in committee, witnesses or solicitors in court, school headmasters or university vice-chancellors at annual prize-giving or graduation ceremonies, Members of Parliament in the House of Commons, or company chairmen at annual general meetings. Even when you have edited out the irrelevant, trivial or banal statements and kept only the important parts of a speech or a debate, you may find that you still have more information than your editor needs.

The answer to the problem is to reduce the over-all length of the remaining material by using a combination of techniques — the techniques of summary, of direct speech, and of reported speech — so that the end result is a good news story with an effective mix of quotes and reported speech.

Techniques of reported speech

The general guideline for changing direct speech to reported, or indirect, speech is that all words in the original speech which suggest nearness of time or place should normally be changed so as to reduce the sense of immediacy of time or place. Thus:

> The editor said: 'I want an answer today. We shall settle this
> issue here and now.'

becomes

> The editor said he wanted an answer that day, and that they
> would settle that issue there and then.

In this representative example the change from direct to
reported speech is brought about by changing key words:
pronouns (the personal pronouns 'I' and 'We' and the demon-
strative pronoun 'this'); verbs (a verb in the present tense,
'want', and a verb in the future tense, 'shall settle'); and
adverbs ('today', 'here' and 'now', or 'here and now' as a
composite adverb). The precise guidelines for the changes are
summarised here.

Pronouns

Pronouns in the first person (I, me, we, us) and the second
person (you) change to the third person unless the change
distorts the sense of the original:

Direct speech	Reported speech
I/me	he/him
you (singular)	he/she — him/her
yours	his/hers
we/us	they/them
you (plural)	they/them
yours	theirs
this/these	that/those

Thus:

Direct speech	Reported speech
He said: 'This is yours.'	He said that was theirs.

But note a statement like this:

> The editor said: 'You and I will have to work late tonight on this
> week's layout.'

The guidelines say that the direct speech pronouns, 'I' and
'you', both change to 'he' in reported speech. But if the

guideline is applied to the example above the result would be absurd:

> The editor said he and he would have to work late that night on that week's layout.

Where there is an ambiguity caused by two or more pronouns then that ambiguity must be eliminated — here and elsewhere in news writing — by using the appropriate noun. In the example above one can assume the editor was talking to his chief reporter, so that the reported speech would be:

> The editor said that he and the chief reporter would have to work late that night on that week's layout.

Verbs

The tense of the verb normally takes one step back into the past. The changes in the verb 'to be' are as follows:

Direct speech	Indirect speech
am/are/is	was/were
shall	should
will	would
may	might
was/were	had been
have been	had been

But note a statement like this:

> The chief officer said: 'Mrs Rosemary Goodison is a member of Glasborough District Council.'

The guidelines say that the present tense 'is' should change to the past tense 'was', but if Mrs Goodison is still a member of the council it would be highly misleading to change the tense of the verb; the change would imply that she was no longer on the council. The example above must therefore be written simply as:

> The chief officer said that Mrs Rosemary Goodison is a member of Glasborough District Council.

Adverbs

Here the guideline is that words suggesting nearness of time or place should normally be changed to remove the sense of proximity. And the reason for the change, of course, is that reported speech is a report of a speech, an account that is given some time after the event and given in a place that may be remote from the original event. Words like 'today', 'yesterday', 'tomorrow', 'tonight', and 'last night' must be precisely qualified if they are to have any clear meaning in a local weekly newspaper.

Some of the common changes are:

Direct speech	Reported speech
now	then
here	there
today	that day
yesterday	the previous day
tomorrow	the following/next day
tonight	that night
last night	the previous night

Once again there are exceptions. Consider this example:

> The speaker said: 'There is no point in regretting the past. All our yesterdays lead us to the here and now.'

That part of the quotation, the popular philosophy of 'All our yesterdays lead us to the here and now', is a permanent, ever present truth and should therefore be left intact. If the normal guidelines were followed then that part of the quotation would not be idiomatic English but would be almost nonsensical:

> All their previous days led them to the there and then.

Similarly, in the folk philosophy, or mock philosophy of:

> 'Never do today what you can put off till tomorrow,' he joked.

the point of the maxim would be blunted by following the guidelines:

> He jokingly said that one should never do that day what one could put off until the next day.

Guidelines and meaning

The guidelines illustrated above are intended to simplify and bring consistency to the task of changing from direct speech to reported speech. If it seems that by following the guidelines you will obscure or distort the meaning of the original, then you must find some other form of words which accurately expresses the meaning of the original in a way that will be understood by your readers.

Exercises in reported speech

Most of the techniques of reported speech are applied to the following example. The techniques of direct speech and summary are also applied because the aim is to write a news story with an effective mix of quotes and reported speech.

From a speech by a regional chairman of the National Farmers' Union:

> 'We in the farming industry are now in the thick of the battle for our survival, and for the future of rural areas in the north. We do not intend to go the way that others have.
>
> 'On some fronts we must fight alone. No one else can make business and investment decisions for us. Management skills and marketing judgements are ours alone to bring to the conduct of our business. And there are always elements of chance, and always the hazards of the weather.
>
> 'If we are not prepared to grasp our opportunities and accept the risks inseparable from the business of farming, then we shouldn't be farming at all.
>
> 'But it is equally important to recognise that decisions of governments — governments around the world — have a major impact on farm incomes, and hence on their ability to invest and to provide employment directly and indirectly too.
>
> 'And so, in the battle for survival, we in the north are entitled to ask what degree of commitment — not just words, but the effective implementation of positive policy measures — what degree of real commitment our Government is prepared to give.'

A news story based on this speech could follow exactly the sequence of the original material, but if we use paragraph three — 'If we are not prepared . . .' — for our intro, we can then follow with the strong quote in the existing first paragraph of the original.

If the news story had to be shorter than the original speech, then the techniques of summary could be applied in paragraph two. Paragraphs four and five could also be summarised and fused into one paragraph.

The present tense of the verb 'to be' is of course justified in the intro of the news story based on the speech.

Michael James   10 March   NFU — 1

If farmers are not prepared to grasp their opportunities and accept the risks of the business, they should not be in farming at all.

That was the message of Mr Alex Thornton, President of the Walls and Dalesmoor Region of the National Farmers' Union (NFU), when he addressed the Dalesmoor branch of the NFU in South Dale last Thursday.

'We in the farming industry are now in the thick of the battle for our survival, and for the future of rural areas in the north,' said Mr Thornton. 'We do not intend to go the way that others have.'

On some fronts the farmers had to fight alone, making business and investment decisions and coping with elements of chance and the hazards of the weather.

'But it is equally important,' he said, 'to recognise that decisions of governments have a major impact on farm incomes. And so, in the battle for survival, we in the north are entitled to ask what degree of real commitment our Government is prepared to give.'

End

Write news stories based on the following speeches.

From a speech at a graduation ceremony last week by Dr Marcus Pryce, the Vice-Chancellor of Glasborough University:

'Try as we may to reverse today's ominous shortfall in the supply of technologists, the initiative may well be doomed for lack of human resources. The nature of the mismatch is well illustrated by drawing your attention to the one obvious difference between graduates in engineering and those in law, or accountancy, or medicine. There are very few women graduates in engineering. Even now in this University, where almost half our 6,500 students are women, only 25 or so study engineering.

'Some say that engineering is not for women. In terms of intellectual capability or academic aptitude, this is nonsense. Medicine is no less demanding in practical skills and scientific background. It all boils down to a reluctance of women to become engineers either because they have been put off by the image of engineering today or because they are largely unaware of the crucial role awaiting for them in that field.

'The public image of engineering is, to some extent, a matter for the profession itself. There is no point in engineers grumbling that their profession lacks the glamour of medicine. They should do something about it. And the best way to add glamour to engineering, to rid the profession once and for all of yesterday's oil-stained image, is to help train and recruit women into the technologies of tomorrow. For let us make no mistake about this. In terms of national survival, the male dominance in technology is potentially disastrous. It means that one half of those school leavers with the qualities to become good engineers are turning their backs on a vital profession which can no longer meet the country's industrial needs because of a chronic shortage of qualified recruits. In that context, if medicine is about caring, engineering is about survival.'

From a speech by Mr Maurice Clamp, chairman of the Walls and Dalesmoor Police Committee. Mr Clamp is referring to the violent conduct of players in a football match between Wallfield United and Glasborough City. The incidents on the field were followed by fighting on the terracing.

'In this particular case before the committee today we are asked to increase the police presence at future games between Wallfield and Glasborough. We all now know that this request stems from the recent incident between rival fans which was sparked off by the behaviour of players of both the Wallfield and the Glasborough clubs, behaviour which in my considered opinion amounted to outright hooliganism every bit as reprehensible as the behaviour on the terraces that afternoon.

'Everyone who has the good of the game at heart was shocked to see players behave in a manner which would certainly have led to their arrest had they behaved in a similar manner off the field of play. To the great shame of the good people of Wallfield and Glasborough, television pictures of the incidents were shown throughout Britain, and our two towns, as well as the game itself, were held up to national ridicule.

'This is intolerable. Players as well as spectators must be made to understand that they are subject to the law. Some of us feel that the culprits on the field were dealt with leniently by their clubs. I personally feel that they should have been charged and brought before a court of law just as the fans were and, if they had been found guilty, they should have been punished just as the fans were.

'I have urged the Chief Constable to adopt a more positive approach in the future. If there is any repetition of such outrageous behaviour on the Wallfield football pitch, I want our Chief Constable to order his officers to arrest the culprits on the spot.'

10

MULTIPLE-TASK EXERCISES

These multiple-task questions require the reader to integrate and apply much of the information and many of the techniques outlined in the previous chapters. Students on journalism courses could treat each question as a team assignment, with two or even three students working on each question.

1 The circulation area of the weekly Wallfield Mercury includes:

A   An active district amateur football league with 20 teams
B   A large college of further education
C   A chamber of commerce with over 100 member firms
D   A large rural area which includes over 20 villages
E   An annual festival of music and the arts which features local amateur clubs and also visiting professional groups

Who would be the most useful contacts for news of these organisations or activities?

How would you establish a working relationship with these contacts?

What advice would you give to each of these contacts about the kind of news he or she could provide?

What advice would you give your contacts, none of whom are professional writers, on the delivery of copy and copy presentation?

What news items or news stories could you reasonably expect from each of your contacts in the course of a year?

What other editorial opportunities — news-features, picture features, interviews, profiles, leaders — could you reasonably expect?

Suggest some form of sponsorship the newspaper could offer to any of the organisations or activities.

Suggest some competitions the newspaper could run, and write the copy for at least one competition.

2 On the day before the weekly Glasborough Gazette goes to press a contact in the Glasborough Division of Chalklands Police Force telephones the editor of the Gazette to tell him that Councillor Harry Dean, a long-serving member of Glasborough District Council and a former mayor of the city, has died suddenly while attending a local government conference in York. Councillor Dean is a widower. Your contact says that Councillor Dean's married daughter, Mrs Elizabeth Dell of Windsor Lane, Glasborough has been informed. Your contact has no further information. The editor knows that relatives of Councillor Dean, other than his daughter, are still living in Glasborough. The editor asks you to act on the information from the police contact.

Suggest three possible sources of information in York. What questions would you ask and what information would you hope to gain?

You call at the home of Mrs Dell. What attitude would you adopt and what preliminary remarks would you make?

Mrs Dell says she is too shocked to discuss her father. How would you respond to this?

You locate another of Councillor Dean's relatives. What questions would you ask about the relative and about the councillor?

What other persons in Glasborough would you approach for information? What would you ask them?

Suggest two possible sources of information within the Gazette offices. What information would you find there and how would you use it?

When you had gathered enough information would you present it as a straight news story? What other form could the story take?

What prominence should the story be given in that week's issue of the Gazette?

What follow-up material could be published in the next issue of the Gazette?

3 The editor of the Wallfield Mercury receives this letter from Mr George Robinson, secretary of Wallfield Town Centre Traders' Association:

> Dear Editor
>
> As the Secretary of Wallfield Town Centre Traders' Association I should like to bring to your readers' attention the growing menace of vandalism in Wallfield town centre.
>
> Many of your readers will have seen evidence of this vandalism in the form of broken shop windows, damaged shop signs, obscene graffiti, broken bottles and even burned-out litter bins.
>
> Traders have repaired the damage promptly so that trade could continue and shoppers would not be inconvenienced more than necessary. If the vandalism persists, however, traders may not be able to afford the repairs and the rising insurance rates. Some traders could even be forced out of business.
>
> Wallfield Police say they are doing what they can and yet the vandalism continues with sickening regularity. The District Council have offered their sympathy but they have offered no practical assistance.
>
> Wallfield Town Centre Traders' Association fear that unless action is taken to stop this crime wave the town centre of Wallfield will become a waste land of empty, boarded-up premises. We also fear that the vandalism will spread to other parts of the town not yet affected.
>
> We appeal to the Police, the Council and the general public to act before it is too late.

The editor of the Mercury decides not to publish the letter immediately. Instead, he asks you to talk to Mr Robinson.

Where should you arrange to meet Mr Robinson? What questions should you ask, and what information would you hope to get?

What other people should you interview and what questions would you ask?

What news angles could you use in your news story?

Write an intro with an appropriate news angle.

Assume you have conducted successful interviews. Write a complete news story.

What photographs could be used to illustrate the story?

Suggest an editorial line that could be taken in a leader on the subject of vandalism in Wallfield town centre.

Write a synopsis for a news-feature or a feature article on the subject. (You could also write the feature in full.)

Outline your ideas for a campaign which the Mercury could run in two or three successive weekly issues.

4 The Glasborough Gazette receives this news release:

Glasborough Heritage Trail

Glasborough District Council have launched a new project which is designed to boost tourism in Glasborough and surrounding areas of Chalklands Valley.

The project, Glasborough Heritage Trail, will also bring wider opportunities for leisure and recreation for local people and will ensure the conservation of historic sites in the city and the countryside.

The Heritage Trail is a carefully planned route which links twenty important landmarks both urban and rural.

Locations in Glasborough include the Cathedral, King's Tower, St Bede's Church, the University campus, and three 18th century cottages in Weavers' Row which have been restored as a craft museum. City sites also include two hotels.

Outside the city the Glasborough Heritage Trail takes in Wycherley Priory, Farnaby Castle, Maudesley Manor and Gardens which are now open to the public for the first time, a five-mile riverside walk along the River Lansing and a new circular walk around Lansing Lake. Other Chalklands Valley sites include three country house hotels.

Mayor of Glasborough Harold Truscott said: 'Glasborough Heritage Trail is a bold and imaginative venture which will promote tourism and conservation in Glasborough and the Chalklands Valley. It will also make our history and our heritage more accessible to local people.'

Mr Roger Andrewes, the Council's Director of Leisure and Recreation, said: 'The project is being marketed throughout Britain and overseas. In association with the British Tourist Authority we have printed 30,000 brochures with maps of the Heritage Trail. A major travel agent has arranged weekend tours of selected sites and week-long tours of all twenty sites on the Heritage Trail.'

Glasborough Heritage Trail is supported by the British Tourist Authority.

end

Further information: Mr Charles Dent, Public Relations Officer, Glasborough District Council.
Telephone: Glasborough 446 2535, ext 980
Home Tel: Glasborough 225 3748

What further information would you seek from the Glasborough public relations officer?

Who else would you interview for the main story, and what questions would you ask?

What further action could you take before writing your story?

Write a news story or a news-feature based on the news release, the interviews and the further action you have taken.

Suggest some ideas for a centre-page spread in the Glasborough Gazette on the subject of the Glasborough Heritage Trail.

Who might be useful contacts for follow-up stories?

What follow-up stories could you reasonably expect to find during a full year?

Suggest some ideas for competitions the Gazette could run on the subject of the Heritage Trail.

5 Mr Henry Warrender, chairman and managing director of Warrender Timber Services, Glasborough, telephones the editor of the Glasborough Gazette and makes this statement:

The Council's Planning Committee met today and rejected my application to purchase the vacant half-acre site alongside my timber storage yard. This means that my expansion plans, which would have brought 30 additional jobs to Glasborough, will have to be scrapped.

The vacant site is owned by the Council. They've had it for the last ten years and they've done nothing with it. I offered them a fair price for it and they turned it down.

I actually attended the planning meeting today but I was there simply as a member of the public and I had no opportunity to speak.

The Director of Planning put forward various arguments. He said the area structure plan did not allow for industrial development in that part of Glasborough, the vacant site was on the edge of a conservation area, and residents in Mayfield Avenue, which is in the conservation area, had lodged objections to my application.

116

The councillors accepted these arguments and rejected my application.

But the real reason, mark you, is that the vacant site has been secretly promised to a new group of property developers, Chalklands Enterprises, who want to build blocks of flats there. I'd like to know who authorised this secret deal, and I think your readers would like to know too.

My company has been providing employment, paying rates and giving a good service in Glasborough for the last twenty years. Now when I try to extend the service and increase employment the Council turns me down and does a secret deal with a bunch of speculators.

I'll be taking further action in this affair. I hope the Gazette will take some action to.

The editor asks you to interview Mr Warrender.

What questions would you ask and what information would you hope to get?

Assume that Mr Warrender gives you reasonably detailed and credible information. You then telephone the director of planning and the chairman of the planning committee.

What manner would you assume and what tactics would you use in your preliminary remarks to these persons?

If the director of planning and the chairman of the committee were both unwilling to comment how would you try to persuade them?

If they still refuse to comment what other councillors or officials would you approach and what tactics would you use in your preliminary remarks?

You then telephone the managing director of Chalklands Enterprises. What tactics would you use in this case? How would you try to persuade the managing director if he were unwilling to talk?

If he refused to comment what further telephone call would you make to Chalklands Enterprises?

What members of the public should you interview? What approach would you adopt and what questions would you ask?

Assume that at the end of your enquiries you have statements only from Mr Warrender and two members of the public.

What news story could the Gazette safely publish? Is there anything in Mr Warrender's original statement which could not be safely published?

APPENDIX

PUBLISHED REFERENCE SOURCES

Many of the volumes listed below are useful reference sources for journalists. Few local newspapers will have all these volumes but most of the volumes will be available in the reference section of the local library.

Dictionaries

Oxford English Dictionary 13 vols (Oxford, Clarendon Press).
Shorter Oxford English Dictionary two vols (Oxford, Clarendon Press).
Concise Oxford Dictionary one vol. (Oxford, Clarendon Press).
Chamber's Twentieth Century Dictionary one vol. (Edinburgh, Chambers).

English Usage

H. W. Fowler: *A Dictionary Of Modern English Usage* (Oxford, Clarendon Press).
David Crystal: *Who Cares About English Usage?* (Harmondsworth, Penguin Books).

Subject Dictionaries

The Oxford series: *The Oxford Companion To English Literature, The Oxford Companion To Music, The Oxford Dictionary Of Quotations* and others.
The extensive Penguin series of subject dictionaries, although less exhaustive than the Oxford, consists of compact and comparatively inexpensive volumes.

Encyclopaedias

The New Encyclopaedia Britannica 30 vols (Chicago/London, Encyclopaedia Britannica).
Everyman's Encyclopaedia 12 vols (London, Dent).

Biographies

Who's Who (London, Black) Biographies, mainly of British and Commonwealth citizens, are revised annually.
The International Who's Who (London, Europa).
Who Was Who (London, Black) Entries are taken mainly from *Who's Who*, with dates of the subjects' deaths.
Dictionary Of National Biography (Oxford, Oxford University Press). Biographies mainly of British, Commonwealth and American persons from early history to the present century.

Specialist Biographies

Dod's Parliamentary Companion (London, Dod's) Biographies of Members of the House of Commons and the House of Lords.
Crockford's Clerical Dictionary (London, Oxford University Press). Details of clergy of the Church of England.
The Bar List Of The United Kingdom (London, Stevens). Details of practising barristers.
The Medical Directory (London, Churchill). Details of medical practitioners registered with the General Medical Council.
Burke's Peerage (London, Burke's). Full title: *Burke's Genealogical And Heraldic History of the Peerage, Baronetage and Knightage.*
Debrett's Peerage And Baronetage (London, Kelly's Directories).

Business and Finance

Who Owns Whom (UK Edition): A Directory Of Parent, Associate and Subsidiary Companies two vols (London, Rosskill). Entries on companies in the UK and Republic of Ireland.

Kompass: Register Of British Industry And Commerce two vols (Croydon, Kompass Publishers) Vol. 1: manufacturers of products and services; Vol. 2 company directors and others.

The Stock Exchange Official Yearbook (Croydon, Thomas Skinner Directories).

Industry, Employment, Society

Report On The Census Of Production (London, H.M.S.O.). Annual reports on British industries.

Report On The Census Of Distribution And Other Services (London, H.M.S.O.). Reports on British retail and service industries.

British Labour Statistics Yearbook (London, H.M.S.O.). Annual employment figures.

Social Trends (London, H.M.S.O.). Annual reports on the British way of life – population, social groups, consumer expenditure, trades unions and other subjects.

News And International Affairs

Hansard. Full title: *Official Reports Of The Parliamentary Debates.* Separate reports for the Commons and the Lords. Includes oral and written answers.

The Statesman's Yearbook (London, Macmillan). Surveys of countries and international organisations.

Keesing's Contemporary Archives (Harlow, Essex, Keesing's). Weekly summaries of world news.

The Annual Register (London, Longman). Annual surveys of regions, countries and subject areas from religion to sport.

Daily Mail Year Book (London, Associated Magazines Ltd). Compact and inexpensive annual

Press And News Media

Benn's Media Directory (formerly *Benn's Press Directory*) two vols (Benn Publications) Vol. 1: Details of all newspapers, magazines and broadcasting organisations in the UK. Vol. 2: Details of the main news media of the world, other than UK.

Willing's Press Guide (Thomas Skinner Directories).

Writers' & Artists' Yearbook (London, A & C Black). Compact annual guide for authors, artists, photographers and others.

Maps, Atlases, Gazetteers

Ordnance Survey maps, printed in various scales, for all areas of Britain.

The Times Atlas Of The World (London, Times Newspapers).

The Times Index–Gazetteer Of The World (London, Times Newspapers).

Bartholomew Gazetteer Of Britain (Edinburgh, Bartholomew).

Gazetteer Of The British Isles (Edinburgh, Bartholomew).

INDEX